Ajit Panicker is a firm believer in the boundless opportunities life offers to discover our true selves. Proudly identifying as a generalist rather than a super-specialist, he contends that super specialization is for unicellular organisms, not for evolved beings like humans.

As a distinguished author, Ajit has penned eleven books, with two becoming best-sellers. His latest work, **"The Failure Code: A Success Formula That Never Fails"** is a notable addition to the self-help genre and an Amazon No. 1 Best-Selling Book.

Beyond his writing, Ajit is an **International Master Trainer & Facilitator specializing in Life Skills, a Motivational Speaker, and a Transformation Coach.** He is also the **founder of The SkillKrafter Academy**, a company dedicated to professional training and coaching services.

Ajit resides in Delhi with his supportive wife, Ratika, and their two children, Paarth and Aarika.

"MY CHILDREN" MY SCHOOL

Everyday Parenting

Ajit Panicker

ARPA PUBLICATIONS

ARPA Publications
Noida, Uttar Pardesh

First published by ARPA Publication in 2025

ISBN: 978-93-341-4750-6

1 0 9 8 7 6 5 4 3 2 1

A Father's Gift

To my dearest Paarth and Aarika

DEDICATION

To the Architects of Tiny Humans

This book is dedicated to all the parents who navigate the whirlwind of "My Children" My School. It's for those who answer endless questions with unwavering patience, those who juggle work, life, and the ever-expanding world of their curious cubs.

You are the first teachers, the builders of character, the ones who instil kindness, responsibility, and a thirst for knowledge. You face tantrums and triumphs, sleepless nights and science fairs, all while shaping the citizens of tomorrow.

May this book be a small tribute to your unwavering dedication. May it remind you that you're not alone in this extraordinary journey, and that the questions, though messy at times, are the seeds of a blossoming future.

Here's to you, the tireless question-answerers, the dream-supporters, the architects of tiny humans who will one day change the world.

EPIGRAPH

"Curiosity is the wick in the lamp of knowledge."

— Confucius

This speaks to the core of the book's theme - the importance of nurturing children's curiosity as they learn and grow. It captures the essence of "My Children, My School," where a parent's role is to guide and support their child's exploration of the world.

CONTENTS

ACKNOWLEDGEMENT

This book wouldn't have found its way into your hands without the support and inspiration of many wonderful people.

First and foremost, to my dearest Paarth and Aarika, thank you for being the reason this book exists. Your endless curiosity, your boundless energy, and your infectious laughter are the fuel that keeps my own sense of wonder alive. This book is a tribute to your adventurous spirits and a promise to always encourage your exploration.

To my wife, my partner, Ratika, in this grand adventure called life, thank you for your unwavering support and patience. You weathered the storms of late-night writing sessions and endless revisions with grace and a smile. Your belief in this project fueled my determination to see it through.

To my parents (if applicable), your own stories of curiosity and exploration planted the seeds for this book. Thank you for nurturing my own sense of wonder and for always encouraging me to ask questions.

To my fellow writers and friends, your insightful feedback and unwavering encouragement kept me going during moments of doubt. Thank you for being a sounding board and a source of inspiration.

And finally, to the countless educators, scientists, and storytellers who have sparked curiosity in children for generations, thank you for reminding us that the world is a fascinating place filled with endless possibilities.

This book is a testament to the power of curiosity, the importance of fostering a love of learning, and the enduring bond between a parent and child. May it inspire young minds to ask questions, explore the world around them, and embark on their own incredible adventures.

■■■

PREFACE

Have you ever been bombarded by a relentless barrage of "whys"? Does bedtime become a negotiation, not a rest? Do you find yourself explaining the meaning of life while making breakfast or while helping them get ready for school? If you answered yes to any (or all) of these questions, then welcome to the wonderful, messy, and often hilarious world of parenthood!

"My Children" My School isn't your typical parenting manual. It's a collection of stories, a reflection on the everyday journey of raising curious little humans. It's a celebration of those moments when the world shrinks to the size of a puddle or a single, fascinating bug. It's a tribute to the tireless parents who navigate the whirlwind of "why" with endless patience and a sprinkle of humour.

This book is for you if you've ever questioned your sanity while explaining the intricacies of gravity or the concept of time zones. It's for you if you've ever felt a surge of pride witnessing your child's insatiable curiosity bloom into a thirst for knowledge. It's for you if you've ever wondered, "Am I doing this right?"

Here, within these pages, you'll find not just stories, but a reminder that you're not alone. You'll find solace in the shared experiences of other parents, a sense of accomplishment in the "aha!" moments of your children, and a renewed appreciation for the power of curiosity.

So, grab a cup of coffee (or a glass of wine, no judgment here!), settle in, and join us on this journey. Let's celebrate the chaos, embrace the questions, and revel in the privilege of nurturing the minds and hearts of our children, our very own tiny schools.

Remember, the symphony of "why" is the sweetest music to a parent's ears, for it signifies a mind that's growing, a spirit that's inquisitive, and a future brimming with possibilities. The journey may be messy, but the rewards are immeasurable.

■■■

INTRODUCTION

Eight years. It feels like yesterday they were bombarding me with questions about puddles and fireflies, and today I'm facing a new set of inquiries – ones that come with a hint of teenage sarcasm and a yearning for independence.

Remember those first few years? The relentless "whys" that echoed through the house, the bedtime negotiations that tested our patience, the simple joy of watching their world expand with every passing day? If you, like me, are a parent of a generation that thrives on questioning, on getting to the heart of "why" things are the way they are, then this book is for you.

"My Children" My School was born from those early years, a collection of stories that captured the messy, beautiful chaos of raising curious minds. But children, much like butterflies, don't stay in their cocoon forever. They emerge, transformed, their questions evolving alongside their wings.

This new title, "My Children" My School reflects this transformation. The wonder hasn't faded, but it's deepened, tinged with a newfound awareness of the world around them. They're questioning not just the mechanics of nature, but the complexities of human interaction, of social justice, of their place in the grand scheme of things.

And let's be honest, these are questions that leave us, as parents, scrambling for answers. How do we navigate conversations about climate change? How do we address the growing pains of social comparison? How do we nurture their curiosity while simultaneously preparing them for the complexities of the world they're about to inherit?

This book isn't a magic solution, a one-size-fits-all guide to raising perfect children. It's a shared journey, a conversation between parents who, like you, are navigating uncharted territory. It's a reminder that the questions, even the difficult ones, are a sign of a mind that's growing, a spirit that's inquisitive, a heart that's yearning to understand.

Within these pages, you'll find stories of triumph and tearful meltdowns, of awkward conversations and moments of pure joy. You'll find solace in the shared experiences of other parents, a sense of accomplishment in the "aha!" moments of your children, and a renewed appreciation for the privilege, and sometimes the sheer terror, of raising a tiny human who's determined to leave their mark on the world.

So, grab a cup of coffee or tea, or maybe juice, settle in, and read. Let's celebrate the chaos, embrace the questions, and revel in the power of curiosity, together. Because even though parenthood can feel like a constant game of catch-up, the rewards – the laughter, the learning, the love – are truly immeasurable.

■■■

FROM SON'S CURIOSITY TO FATHER'S LEGACY

How "My School, My Father" Paves the Way for "My Children" My School

My School "My Father", my first book laid the groundwork for what has now become **"My Children" My School.** The first book centered around Mr. Nair, his wife, and their children, Prashantan and Smitha. It explored Mr. Nair's role in guiding his children's intellectual and moral development through everyday conversations.

Here's a breakdown of the themes that bridge the two books:

- **The Power of Everyday Moments:** Both books highlight how seemingly ordinary moments can become valuable teaching opportunities. Mr. Nair uses breakfast conversations, bedtime stories, and everyday situations to answer his children's questions and instil important life lessons. Prashantan, in **"My Children" My School** likely uses a similar approach with his own twins.
- **Fostering Curiosity:** Both books celebrate the importance of curiosity as a driving force for learning. Mr. Nair encourages Prashantan and Smitha to ask questions and explore the world around them. Prashantan, as a father, likely strives to do the same with Paarth and Aarika.
- **The Parent as Teacher:My School "My Father"** emphasizes the crucial role parents play in shaping their children's early education. Similarly, **"My Children" My School** acknowledges the ongoing responsibility of parents to guide and support their children's intellectual and emotional growth.

The Evolution of a Father:"My Children" My School picks up where the first book left off, showcasing Prashantan's journey as a father. He's no longer the curious child seeking answers, but a grown man grappling with the challenges of raising inquisitive twins, Paarth and Aarika. The book delves into the questions they ask as they grow from age 5 to 9, questions that are likely more complex and nuanced than those Prashantan and Smitha asked in their younger years.

The Legacy of Mr. Nair: While Mr. Nair may not be physically present, his influence is likely woven into the fabric of **"My Children" My School.** Prashantan, shaped by his own experience with his father, might subconsciously use some of the same techniques Mr. Nair employed. The book could explore how Prashantan honours his father's memory by fostering a love of learning and open communication with his own children.

In essence, **"My Children" My School** is a continuation of the story that began in **My School "My Father".** It offers a glimpse into the next generation, showcasing the challenges and joys of raising curious children in a world vastly different from the one Mr. Nair navigated. Both books, however, celebrate the enduring power of parental love, communication, and the importance of nurturing a child's natural curiosity.

■■■

CHAPTER 1

WHY IS THE SKY BLUE?

Paarth looked out the window, his eyebrow wrinkled in concentration. The afternoon sun was high in the sky, a dazzling spread of bright blue. "Papa!" he called, his voice spiked with wonder, "Why is the sky blue? It's not like my room, which can be green or yellow depending on the lamp I turn on!"

Aarika peeked over his shoulder, her eyes sparkling with curiosity. "Yeah, Papa," she seconded him, "and sometimes the sky is orange and purple at sunset. Why does it change colours?"

Their father, Prashantan, ruffled their hair with a gentle smile playing on his lips. "Ah, excellent questions! The sky looks blue because of a magical game of light and air. Imagine sunlight as a rainbow, with all the colours hiding inside it," he began, his voice taking on a captivating tone.

Paarth's eyes widened. Rainbows were his favourite! Aarika bounced on her toes, eager to hear more.

"When sunlight reaches Earth," their father continued, "it bumps into tiny particles in the air. These sneaky air molecules scatter the sunlight in all directions. But blue light, being the smallest and most energetic, scatters the most. That's why we see a big, beautiful blue sky most of the time!"

Aarika gasped. "So, the air is like a giant glass, separating the sunlight colours?"

Their father smiled with amusement. "Not exactly a glass, but it does something similar to what a Prism does. It separates the colours, letting the blue light shine through the most."

Paarth's eyebrow furrowed in thought. "Papa, what's a prism?"

Their father, slightly taken aback, replied, "I'll explain it to you in detail later. For now, just think of it as a type of glass."

But what about sunsets, Papa? Why are the colours different then?"

Their father's smile turned a little thoughtful. "Ah, sunsets are a different kind of magic. When the sun dips low in the sky, its light has to travel through more air. The blue light gets scattered away, leaving the red and orange colours behind. That's what paints the sky in those fiery shades we see at the end of the day."

He knelt before them, his eyes twinkling. "Isn't nature amazing, my little explorers? The sky is a giant canvas, painted with different colours depending on the time of day and the tricks sunlight plays with the air."

Paarth and Aarika exchanged excited glances. The sky wasn't just blue anymore; it was a place of wonder, filled with light and a touch of magic. They couldn't wait to explore it more, their imaginations already soaring through the vast expanse.

■■■

CHAPTER 2

HOW DO AIRPLANES FLY?

Paarth pressed his nose against the cool airplane window, his eyes wide with a mixture of fascination and anxiety. Below them, the world shrunk into a miniature landscape of green squares and silver ribbons – houses and roads that once seemed so big were now like tiny toys.

"Papa," he whispered, his voice barely audible over the soft hum of the engines, "How do these giant planes stay up there? It doesn't seem fair, they're so heavy!"

His father, sensing Paarth's wonder and a hint of fear, smiled reassuringly. "Ah, that's a question that's puzzled people for centuries! But fear not, there's a secret behind how airplanes fly, and it has something to do with something invisible called 'lift.'

Paarth's frown melted into curiosity. "Lift? Like when I help you lift the heavy boxes?"

"Not quite," his father giggled, "but the idea is similar. Airplanes have these amazing wings, designed like giant curved birds. As the airplane races forward, the air whooshes over and under the wings." He gestured with his hands, mimicking the flow of air.

Aarika, who had been quietly listening, tilted her head. "But wouldn't the air just push the plane down, Papa?"She frowned slightly in contemplation.

Her father's eyes sparkled. "That's a great question, Aarika! The clever part is, the shape of the wings makes the air travel faster over the top than the bottom. This creates a funny situation – the air pressure on top of the wing is lower than underneath!"

Paarth's gasp echoed in the small cabin. "Lower pressure? So, it's like a giant invisible hand pushing the airplane up?"

His father grinned. "Exactly! That's a lift in action! It's like the air itself is holding the airplane up, just like you held that balloon yesterday that wouldn't touch the ground."

Aarika's eyes flew open in sudden understanding. "So, it's like when I hold my hand out the car window, and it feels like it's flying? It's the same invisible force?"

"Absolutely! You've got it!" Her father gently played with her hair."Airplanes use powerful engines to zoom forward, which creates the perfect whoosh of air needed for lift. It's a magical combination of science and wonder that allows these giant machines to soar through the sky!"

Paarth stared back out the window, a newfound appreciation blooming in his chest. Those enormous airplanes weren't just machines anymore; they were symbols of human ingenuity, defying gravity and taking flight on invisible currents. A tiny spark ignited within him, a dream taking flight alongside the airplane – a dream of soaring among the clouds himself, one day.

■■■

CHAPTER 3

WHY DO WE HAVE TO GO TO SCHOOL?

Aarika sunk dramatically in her seat, kicking her legs listlessly against the floor. “But Papa,” she wailed, her voice thick with disappointment, “It's a beautiful day outside! Can't we just stay home and play UNO or Monopoly or play in the park?”

Paarth, ever the logician, butted in, “Yeah, school seems kind of pointless sometimes. Why can't we just learn stuff at home with you? You know way more than Ms. Monika about dinosaurs!”

Prashantan, used to their occasional Monday morning protests, smiled. He knelt before them, his warm eyes crinkling at the corners. “I understand how you feel,” he admitted, his voice softening. “Sometimes, school can feel like a chore, a place where fun goes to die.”

Aarika's bottom lip trembled. “Do we really have to go and learn all that boring stuff about fractions and spelling?”

Her father brushed away a tear that escaped her eye. “There will definitely be times when schoolwork feels challenging or uninteresting. But trust me, the things you learn in school are like magical tools that unlock a whole new world of understanding.”

He gestured towards the window where fluffy clouds drifted across the blue sky. “Remember yesterday, when you were so curious about how airplanes fly? You learned about lift and air pressure, right?”

Paarth’s eyes lit up. “Yeah! And how the wings are like giant bird wings!”

“Exactly!” Their father beamed. “Those things you learned in science class made you think more about it and you came enquiring to me. Was School, not the place where it started? School is like a treasure chest filled with knowledge waiting to be discovered. It may not always be sunshine and rainbows, but the things you learn can take you on incredible adventures, just like a trip on an airplane!"

Aarika pondered this for a moment, a flicker of curiosity replacing her earlier dejection. "So, school helps us unlock the secrets of the world, like how airplanes fly and why the sky is blue?"

"Absolutely! And not just those things," their father continued, his voice filled with enthusiasm. "You'll learn about history, different cultures, amazing stories from all over the world. You'll even discover how to write your own stories and express your ideas!"

A tiny spark ignited in Aarika's eyes. Maybe school wasn't just about boring lessons after all. Maybe it was a key to unlocking a universe of knowledge, a place where she could learn to create and explore. With a newfound determination, she grabbed her backpack, a hint of butterflies fluttering in her stomach. School wasn't just about lessons anymore; it was an exciting adventure waiting to unfold.

■■■

CHAPTER 4

HOW DO ANIMALS TALK TO EACH OTHER?

Paarth squatted by the window, his nose pressed against the cool glass. He watched intently as a family of pigeons, heads bobbing, waddled across the park, their wings occasionally flashing in the morning sunlight.A constant cooing echoed through the park, a low thrum that seemed to carry a hidden message.

"Papa," Paarth called, his voice filled with wonder, "What are the pigeons saying to each other? They sound so busy!"

His father smiled, a knowing glint in his eyes. "Ah, those pigeons are having a lively conversation! But unlike us, they don't use words. Animals have their own special languages, a secret code of chirps, clicks, and whistles."

Aarika, got curious, bounced on the balls of her feet. "So, it's like a secret code that only animals understand?"

"Exactly!" her father chuckled. "Each chirp, each tweet, each wag of the tail carries a meaning. It's their way of talking to each other, sharing information about food, danger, or even potential mates."

Paarth frowned his nose in concentration. "But how do we know what they're saying, Papa?"

"We may not understand every chirp or wiggle," his father admitted, "but scientists have spent years studying animal communication. They're slowly cracking the code, learning the meanings behind the sounds and gestures."

He gestured towards the pigeons outside. "Listen closely. Do you hear that low, persistent cooing? That probably means they've found some dropped crumbs or scraps and are calling the others over."

A wide grin spread across Paarth's face. He strained his ears, focusing on the pigeons' communication. With newfound awareness, he imagined he could almost understand the meaning behind their coos, the subtle shifts in tone and rhythm.

"Wow," Aarika breathed, her eyes sparkling with fascination. "Our cat's meows must be her way of telling us things too, right?"

"Absolutely!" her father confirmed. "A low, rumbling purr probably means she's content and happy. A loud meow might be her way of asking for food or attention. By learning their language, we can understand our animal friends much better."

Suddenly, the backyard transformed into a busy marketplace of chirps, squawks, and rustling leaves. A crow cawed a warning, a squirrel chattered in alarm, and a butterfly flitted by, its wings a silent message in the dance of the breeze. The world around them seemed to come alive with a hidden symphony of communication.

Paarth's heart swelled with a newfound appreciation for the natural world. It wasn't just a collection of creatures; it was a vibrant embroidery woven with the threads of countless languages, each one a secret waiting to be unraveled. The desire to learn more about these hidden conversations bloomed within him, a seed waiting to take root in the fertile ground of his curiosity. The backyard wasn't just a place to play anymore; it was a gateway to a whole new world waiting to be explored, a world where even the smallest creatures had stories to tell.

■■■

CHAPTER 5

WHERE DO BABIES COME FROM?

Aarika squirmed on the edge of the sofa, her eyebrows furrowed in a way that usually meant a big question was brewing. Her eyes, wide and curious, darted between her father and the picture book they had just been reading, filled with images of happy families and bouncing babies.

"Papa," she whispered hesitantly, "Where do these little babies come from?"

Her father's smile softened, and he knelt before her, his eyes meeting hers with a warmth that instantly calmed any anxieties. "Ah, Aarika," he said gently, "That's a very important question, one that deserves a thoughtful answer."

He glanced at Paarth, who had also become attentive, his ears twitching with curiosity. Aarika and Paarth were at that age – not quite little anymore, but still innocent enough for the world to hold a constant stream of fascinating mysteries.

"See, Aarika," he continued, his voice taking on a hushed, almost reverent tone, "Families are created with a very special kind of magic."

Aarika's eyes widened further. Magic? This was even better than she'd hoped for!

"It all starts with a mommy and a daddy who love each other very much," her father explained, placing a hand over his heart. "That love creates a tiny spark, a wish for a new life to join their family."

He gestured to his stomach. "Inside the mommy's tummy, there's a special place called a womb, all warm and cozy, just waiting for something amazing to happen."

Paarth, usually the more impatient one, piped up, "But how does the baby get in there, Papa?"

Her father chuckled. "That's where the magic truly begins, Paarth. The mommy has a special cell, called an egg, and the daddy has another special cell, much smaller, called a sperm. Imagine these cells like tiny puzzle pieces, each with a special part of the love and magic that mommy and daddy share."

Aarika frowned as she tried to understand the strange picture her father was describing.

"Sometimes," he continued, his voice dropping to a conspiratorial whisper, "When the mommy and daddy share a special hug, filled with all that love, the daddy's sperm can travel on a magical journey to meet the mommy's egg."

Paarth gasped. "A journey? Inside mommy?"

"Exactly!" Her father winked. "And if they meet in that cozy womb, something incredible happens. The sperm and the egg join together, like two perfect puzzle pieces clicking into place. That's when the magic happens, Paarth. That's when a new life begins to grow!"

Aarika's hand flew to her mouth, her eyes wide with wonder. A baby, a real, live baby, started as a tiny spark of love that grew into a magical puzzle. It was far more fascinating than anything she could have imagined.

"So, that's why Mama's tummy got big before we were born?" Paarth asked, his voice filled with a newfound reverence.

Her father's smile widened. "Exactly, my little adventurer! You and Aarika both grew big and strong inside your Mama's tummy, surrounded by all that love and magic, until you were ready to join our family and share in the adventure of life."

Aarika leaned back against her father, a sense of awe washing over her. The world felt a little different now, filled with a hidden magic that connected families and brought new life into existence. The next time she looked at a baby, she wouldn't just see a cute face; she would see a miracle, a testament to the power of love and the wonder of creation.

■■■

CHAPTER 6

WHY DO I HAVE TO SHARE MY TOYS?

Aarika clutched her beloved stuffed unicorn, Twilight Sparkle, to her chest, her tri-colour mane glinting defiantly in the afternoon sun. Across the room, Paarth eyed Twilight Sparkle with undisguised longing, his own frog soft toy, one that he had named Silky, looking decidedly worse for wear in comparison.

"Papa," Aarika wailed, her voice thick with possessiveness, "Paarth wants to play with Twilight Sparkles, but she's mine! I don't want to share!"

A familiar pang of frustration shot through Paarth's chest. Sharing, especially when it came to Twilight Sparkles' magical adventures, was a constant battleground between them. Their father, ever the peacekeeper, knelt before them, a gentle smile on his face.

"Ah," he began, his voice warm and soothing,"sharing can be tricky sometimes, especially when it comes to our favourite toys. Twilight Sparkles seems like a very special friend to you, Aarika."

Aarika nodded vigorously, burying her face deeper into Twilight Sparkles' sequined mane. She wasn't just a toy; she was her confidante, her brave knight who vanquished imaginary dragons and explored enchanted forests. The thought of letting anyone else touch her sent shivers down her spine.

"But sharing isn't just about giving away something you love," her father continued, his eyes twinkling with understanding. "Sometimes, it's about letting someone else experience the joy you feel."

He gestured towards Paarth, whose bottom lip trembled slightly. "Imagine, Paarth could take Twilight Sparkles on a daring rescue mission too! Maybe they could save a princess from a grumpy troll together. Wouldn't that be an amazing adventure?"

Paarth's eyes lit up at the prospect. A grumpy troll? That was way more exciting than anything his Silky Froggy could handle! A tiny seed of doubt began to sprout in Aarika's mind. Maybe sharing Twilight Sparkles wouldn't be so bad after all. Maybe it could even lead to a more epic adventure?

"But what if she gets dirty or ripped?" Aarika worried, her voice laced with a hint of worry.

Her father chuckled. "That's a good point! We can always set some ground rules," he suggested. "Maybe Paarth can only play with Twilight Sparkles for a little while, and we can be extra careful. After all, a brave knight like Twilight Sparkles must be strong for his many adventures!"

The idea of Twilight Sparkles embarking on even grander quests, with Paarth by her side, slowly chipped away at Aarika's resistance. A tiny spark of generosity flickered within her. Maybe, just maybe, sharing Twilight Sparkles wouldn't be the end of the world. In fact, it could be the beginning of a whole new chapter in their playtime saga.

With a deep breath and a hesitant nod, Aarika loosened her grip on Twilight Sparkles. The act felt a little scary, like letting go of a precious secret. But as Paarth's face broke into a wide grin, and he gently took Twilight Sparkles from her hands, a new emotion bloomed in Aarika's chest – the warmth of sharing something special and the joy of creating a shared adventure with her brother.

■■■

CHAPTER 7

WHY DO YOU AND MUMMA KISS?

A blanket of twilight had settled over the house, casting long shadows that danced on the walls. Aarika and Paarth snuggled close to their parents on the couch, the warmth a comforting shield against the approaching darkness. A question, whispered like a secret, hung in the air.

"Papa," Paarth began, his voice barely above a murmur, his eyes rushing between his parents' faces, "Why do you and Mumma kiss sometimes?"

Aarika, with curiousity, asked, "Yeah, it looks funny! Like you're sharing a secret snack."

Their parents exchanged a smile, a silent conversation passing between them. A warmth bloomed in their eyes, a secret language only love could understand.

"Well," their father began, his voice gentle, "Kissing isn't just about funny faces, Aarika. It's a way to show something very special."

He took their mother's hand in his, his fingers intertwining with hers. Aarika watched, mesmerized, as a soft smile touched her mother's lips.

"See," their father continued, "When Mama and I kiss, it's like a little whisper between us. It says, 'I love you,' 'I care about you,' and 'I'm happy to be here with you.'

Paarth's eyebrow furrowed in concentration. "But you already say those things out loud sometimes."

"That's true, Paarth," their mother chimed in, her voice soft and melodic. "But sometimes, words aren't enough. A kiss is a special kind of hug, a way to show our love without needing to speak."

She leaned closer to their father, their foreheads touching for a fleeting moment. Aarika felt a strange fluttering in her stomach, a warmth that spread from her chest to her fingertips. It wasn't funny at all; it felt...important.

"It's like a secret handshake, but for grown-ups?" Paarth added, his eyes wide with newfound understanding.

Their father smiled. "Not exactly a handshake, but yes there is a secret involved, the secret of love. A kiss is a way to share that secret with someone special."

Aarika pondered on it for a moment, the image of her parents' kiss replaying in her mind. It wasn't just a funny face anymore; it was a symbol, a whispered promise spoken in the language of love. A shy smile tugged at the corners of her lips. Maybe, just maybe, she understood a little bit more about the grown-up world now.

"So, if we want to show you we love you," she began hesitantly, her eyes sparkling with a newfound tenderness, "Can we give you a kiss too on your lips?"

Their parents' faces broke into radiant smiles, warm and full of love. "We'd love that more than anything, Aarika, but would prefer the kiss on the cheeks" their father replied, pulling her close for a hug.

As Aarika nestled into her father's embrace, a newfound sense of warmth bloomed within her. The world felt a little brighter, a little fuller of love, now that she understood the secret language of kisses.

■■■

CHAPTER 8

WHY DO YOU GO TO WORK EVERY DAY?

A shadow of disappointment flickered across Aarika's face as she watched her father pull on his tie, the crisp fabric a stark contrast to the playful pyjamas she still wore. "Papa," she mumbled, her voice thick with a sadness that tugged at his heartstrings, "Why do you and mumma have to go to work every day? Can't you guys stay and play hide and seek with us?"

Paarth, ever the pragmatist, added to it, his eyebrows furrowed in a way that mirrored his father's morning struggles. "Yeah, work sounds boring. Why can't you just stay home and build towers with the building block games we have or read us stories?"

Their father's smile faltered for a moment, a flicker of longing crossing his features. He knelt before them, his eyes filled with a warmth that could melt away any disappointment.

"I know work doesn't always seem like the most exciting adventure," he admitted, his voice gentle. "But going to work is important, just like school is important for you."

Aarika's bottom lip trembled. "But school isn't about earning money," she argued, her voice barely a whisper.

"That's true, Aarika," her father explained, brushing a stray strand of hair from her forehead. "The money I earn from work helps us buy things we need, like food to fill our stomach, a cozy house to keep us comfortable, and even the books you love to read."

He gestured around the room, his eyes filled with a quiet pride. "See all these things that make our life comfortable and happy? Work helps make that possible."

Paarth, got curious, tilted his head. "But why can't you just use magic to make all those things appear?"

A chuckle escaped their father's lips. "If only it were that easy, Paarth! But the world works a little differently. Many people work hard at different jobs, like doctors, teachers, and builders, and that's how we all get the things we need."

Aarika pondered this for a moment, a spark of understanding flickering in her eyes. "So, your work is like your own special adventure? You use your skills to help others, and that helps us too?"

"Exactly, Aarika!" Her father beamed. "My work might not be about slaying dragons or sailing the high seas," he added with a wink, "but it's my way of contributing to our family and making the world a better place, even in a small way."

Paarth, usually restless, seemed thoughtful. "So, when you come home from work, you're like a tired but triumphant hero?"

A wave of warmth washed over their father. "Maybe not a hero, Paarth," he said, pulling them both into a hug, "But someone who's happy to be back with his favourite two adventurers and the mother of these explorers. And who knows, maybe one day you'll both find your own special ways to contribute to the world, just like me."

The disappointment that had clouded their faces earlier had melted away, replaced by a newfound understanding and a spark of pride. Maybe work wasn't the enemy after all. Maybe it was just another part of the grand adventure called life, a way to build a future filled with love, laughter, and the joy of being a family.

■■■

CHAPTER 9

HOW DID YOU AND MUMMA MEET?

Aarika curled up on the sofa, her chin resting on her knees. Her eyes, wide and full of curiosity, were fixed on her father. Paarth, usually a ball of boundless energy, sat uncharacteristically still, mirroring his sister's rapt attention.

"Papa," Aarika began, her voice barely a whisper, "How did you and Mumma meet? Was it like a fairytale, with a damsel in distress and a brave soldier?"

A warm smile bloomed on their father's face, a smile that crinkled the corners of his eyes and reached all the way to his heart. He settled beside them, the familiar scent of his cologne a comforting presence.

"Well, Aarika," he chuckled, "There weren't any dragons or damsels in distress, but our story has its own kind of magic."

Paarth scrunched his nose in mock disappointment. "No dragons? But that's the best part!"

Their father ruffled his hair playfully. "Maybe not dragons, Paarth," he conceded, "But there was definitely a spark, a feeling that something special was about to happen."

He took a deep breath, his eyes drifting back to a time etched in his memory. "Mumma and I met for the first time in College while we enrolled in our Masters in Business Management," he explained. "I saw your Mumma for the first time, as she introduced herself on the stage. Something that I got hitched bywas her unique talent for singing the Hindi-Bollywood songs in reverse. That was something. I must say."

Aarika's eyes widened. "College. Just like it happens in movies? And how does Mumma sing in reverse? I am going to make her sing for me, as well."

Her father chuckled again. "Maybe not exactly like the movies, Aarika, but it was pretty close. We started talking, and it felt like we'd known each other forever. We shared our love for family, our passion for adventure, our dreams of who we want to be and a way of making each other laugh until our sides ached."

Paarth, captivated by the tale, leaned in closer. "So, you just knew she was the one, right then and there?"

Their father's smile softened. "Not quite, Paarth. It wasn't like a bolt of lightning from the sky. But there was a connection, a feeling of warmth and comfort that grew stronger with each conversation, each shared story, each laugh with every date we went on."

He gestured between them. "Just like you build a tower with blocks, one piece at a time, my friendship with Mumma grew stronger. We built a foundation of trust, understanding, and shared dreams."

Aarika's brow furrowed in concentration. "So, being friends first is important?"

"Absolutely, Aarika! Friendship is like the roots of a tree, strong and steady. It gives love a place to grow and flourish."

Paarth, usually restless, remained excited. "And then what happened? Did you propose on a mountaintop at sunset?"

Their father laughed, a rich sound that filled the room. "No mountaintops, Paarth," he admitted, winking. "But there was a park, a beautiful bouquet of red roses, and a question that came from the very bottom of my heart. It was a little dramatic"

Aarika sighed dramatically. "Ah, dramatic. Why was it dramatically romantic?"

Their father wrapped his arm around them both, pulling them close. "It was more than just romantic, Aarika. It was the beginning of a beautiful journey, a journey that led us to parenthood, to you two amazing little adventurers."

He looked into their eyes, each one a reflection of his own love story. "So, you see," he concluded, his voice filled with tenderness, "Our love story may not have started with a bang, but it grew into something strong, something true, something that brought you both into the world."

A warm silence settled over them, a silence filled with the unspoken language of love and family. The idea of their parents having been friends first, building a foundation of laughter and shared dreams, filled Aarika and Paarth with a new appreciation for their bond. Maybe, just maybe, their own friendships held the seeds of future love stories waiting to bloom.

■■■

CHAPTER 10

DO YOU HAVE A FAVOURITE CHILD?

Aarika clutched her stuffed unicorn, Twilight Sparkles, a flicker of worry dancing in her eyes. She loved her brother dearly, but sometimes, a tiny, nagging voice whispered doubts in her ear.

"Papa," she began, her voice barely above a whisper, "Do you...do you have a favourite child?"

The question hung heavy in the air, a tiny bomb thrown into their comfortable afternoon. Paarth, usually a whirlwind of boundless energy, froze mid-sentence, his toy truck clattering to the floor with a forgotten thud.

Their father, ever perceptive, knelt before them, his warm brown eyes searching their faces. Aarika felt a lump form in her throat, the unspoken fear threatening to spill over.

"A favourite child?" he repeated slowly, his voice laced with a gentle curiosity. "Why would you ask that, Aarika?"

Aarika, her lower lip trembling, mumbled something about wanting to be the best, the one who made him proudest. Paarth, eyes wide and mirroring his sister's worry, asked too, "Did we do something wrong?"

Their father's heart ached at the sight of their vulnerability. He pulled them both into a tight embrace, the warmth of his love a silent reassurance.

"Oh, my precious little ones," he murmured, his voice thick with emotion. "The idea of a favourite child is simply not true. My love for you both is like the sun – it shines equally on all things, warming them with the same intensity."

He pulled back slightly, his gaze fixed on Aarika's tear-filled eyes. "You, Aarika, are my bright and curious ray of sunshine. You fill our world with grace, poise, calm and sanity with your cute voice and serenity of your personality."

A tiny smile tugged at the corner of Aarika's lips. Maybe she wasn't just a shadow of her brother. Maybe she had her own special way of shining.

Her father turned to Paarth, his hand ruffling the boy's messy hair. "And you, Paarth, are my little explorer, always ready for an adventure. Your adventurous spirit and boundless energy keep us on our toes, but they also remind us to embrace the joy in the simple things."

Paarth's chest puffed out with pride. Maybe being the adventurous one wasn't a bad thing after all.

"You see," their father continued, his voice filled with unwavering conviction, "You both bring different joys, different challenges, and a unique kind of love into our life as parents. It's like a beautiful melody – each note adds its own special sound, but together, they create a harmony that fills our heart with happiness."

Aarika and Paarth sat in comfortable silence, their anxieties replaced by a newfound understanding. Their love for their father wasn't a competition; it was a symphony, a beautiful composition where each of them played an irreplaceable part.

"So, we're both your favourite adventurers?" Paarth finally asked, a hopeful glint in his eyes.

Their father laughed, a sound that chased away the last remnants of doubt. "Absolutely! You're both my favourite adventurers, my favourite storytellers, my favourite cuddle buddies. My love for each of you is a treasure, unique and irreplaceable."

With hearts brimming with love and a renewed sense of security, Aarika and Paarth leaned back into their father's embrace, ready to face any adventure, knowing that their love for each other, and their father's love for them, would be the guiding light on their journey.

■■■

CHAPTER 11

WHY DO LEAVES CHANGE COLOUR IN THE AUTUMN?

A crisp autumn breeze swirled through the park, sending a shower of colourful leaves cascading down around them. Aarika and Paarth, bundled in cozy wears, danced and twirled amidst the swirling foliage, their laughter echoing through the crisp air. But amidst the playful chaos, a question bloomed in Aarika's mind.

"Papa," she called, her voice laced with wonder as she held up a fiery red leaf, "Why do the leaves change colour? They look like they're all dressed up for a party!"

Paarth, always the practical one, added, "Yeah, why can't they just stay green all year long? Although green is boring, and these colours are pretty cool!"

Their father smiled, his eyes twinkling with the same warmth that surrounded them. He went closer to them, gathering a handful of colourful leaves in his own hands – a vibrant bouquet of nature's transformation.

"Well, Aarika," he began, his voice gentle, "These changing colours are a secret message from the trees. They're getting ready for a very important event – a long winter rest."

Aarika's eyes widened. "A slumber? Like we do at night?"

"Not quite like sleep, Aarika," their father explained, "But more like a deep rest. Winter brings cold winds and less sunlight, making it hard for the trees to find the food they need."

"He gestured towards a neem leaf, its slightly yellowed edges a stark contrast to the vibrant green of summer. 'See this change in color? It's like a special transformation the tree undergoes. The bright green you see during the summer is due to chlorophyll, which helps the leaves make food from sunlight.

But as the weather cools down, the amount of sunlight decreases, and the chlorophyll starts to break down."

Paarth's brow creased in thought. "I understand the green fading, but how does the red appear?"

"That's the clever part, Paarth! Red, orange, and yellow colours have always been hiding inside the leaves, but they were masked by the stronger green chlorophyll. When the green fades, these hidden colours finally get to shine!"

Aarika's eyes sparkled with newfound understanding. "So, it's like a magic trick? The green disappears, and then poof, there are new colours!"

Their father laughed, the sound as warm as the sunbeams filtering through the changing leaves. "Not quite magic, Aarika, but a clever way for the trees to prepare for winter. They conserve their energy by getting rid of the green chlorophyll they don't need anymore, and they show off their hidden beauty at the same time."

Paarth, always the adventurer, bounced on the balls of his feet. "So, the trees are getting ready for a big adventure too? Like a long sleep before they wake up for spring?"

Their father smiled, pulling them both into a hug. "Exactly, Paarth! Autumn is a time for the trees to say goodbye to summer and get ready for their winter rest. And just like the trees, we all need times to rest and recharge, so we can be ready for our own spring adventures."

As they continued their walk through the park, the fallen leaves no longer seemed like scattered debris, but like tiny flags, a colourful celebration of nature's changing seasons. Aarika and Paarth skipped alongside their father, their hearts filled with a newfound appreciation for the hidden messages whispered by the trees, a reminder that change, like the vibrant hues of fall, could be a beautiful part of life's grand adventure.

■■■

CHAPTER 12

HOW DOES RAIN HAPPEN?

A relentless drumming echoed on the rooftop, a sound that usually filled Paarth with a sense of cozy adventure. But today, a different emotion clouded his face – frustration. He stomped over to the window, his nose pressed against the cold glass, watching raindrops race down the pane.

"Papa," he grumbled, his voice stifled by the downpour, "Why does it have to rain all day? We can't even go outside and play!"

Aarika, always the dreamer, perched on the window seat beside him. Her gaze, however, wasn't fixed on the relentless rain, but on the swirling clouds above. They seemed to churn and roil, pregnant with an unseen energy.

"Maybe," she whispered, her voice laced with wonder, "The rain isn't just falling down. Maybe it's the clouds crying."

Their father, the patient listener, smiled from behind them. He pulled up a chair, the familiar scent of his cologne a comforting presence in the storm-filled room.

"Crying clouds, huh, Aarika?" he chuckled. "That's a very poetic way to look at it. But the rain isn't exactly tears, though it does have a story to tell."

Paarth, his frustration momentarily forgotten, turned towards his father, his eyes wide with curiosity. "A story? What kind of story?"

Their father gestured towards the window. "The story of rain is all about a never-ending journey, a grand adventure called the water cycle."

He pulled out a book filled with colourful pictures, a familiar friend on rainy days. As he opened it, Aarika and Paarth rushed closer, their imaginations ignited.

"Imagine," their father began, his voice warm and inviting, "The sun as a giant lamp, shining down on the Earth. Its warmth touches the oceans, rivers, and lakes, turning the water into a magical mist that floats up into the sky."

Aarika's eyes sparkled. "Like Mr. Sparkles disappearing in a puff of smoke during our magic shows?"

Their father laughed. "Not quite like smoke, Aarika, but kind of like magic. This invisible mist is called water vapor, and it rises higher and higher, meeting the cool air up there."

He pointed to a picture in the book, a fluffy white cloud drifting across a blue sky. "The cool air makes the water vapor huddle together, forming tiny droplets, like millions of teardrops clinging to each other."

Paarth wrinkled his nose. "But why would the water vapor cry?"

"It's not crying, Paarth," their father explained. "It's just that the droplets are getting too heavy to stay up in the sky any longer. So, they join hands and fall back down to Earth, splashing down as rain."

Aarika gasped. "So, the rain is like all the tiny droplets holding hands and jumping down together?"

Their father smiled. "Exactly, Aarika! And when the rain falls on the ground, it soaks into the earth, fills up rivers and lakes, and even travels underground, waiting for the sun to come back and start the whole adventure all over again."

As they continued reading, the rain outside no longer seemed like a nuisance, but a vital part of a grand story. A story of journeys, transformations, and the never-ending circle of life. Aarika and Paarth looked out the window with newfound appreciation, watching the rain paint glistening streaks down the glass. Maybe staying in wasn't so bad after all. After all, they had a front-row seat to nature's grand water adventure.

■■■

CHAPTER 13

WHY DO WE HAVE DIFFERENT SEASONS?

Aarika stared out the window, her eyebrows focused on the things unfolding outside. The world outside was ablaze with the fiery hues of summer – lush green leaves, vibrant flowers, and a relentless sun that seemed to paint the sky with its warmth. But amidst the beauty, a question bloomed in her mind, a nagging curiosity that demanded an answer.

"Papa," she asked softly, "Why do the seasons change? Why is it so hot in the summer and so cold in the winter?"

Paarth, sprawled on the floor with his toy trucks, chimed in without looking up. "Yeah, it's like someone keeps changing the settings on the giant weather machine!"

Aarika giggled at the image, but their father knelt before them, his eyes twinkling with the promise of an explanation.

"Well, Aarika," he began, his voice gentle, "the answer to your question has to do with a grand cosmic dance – a dance between the Earth and the sun."

He spread his arms wide, his fingers brushing the air as if tracing an invisible path. "Imagine the Earth is like a giant spinning top, tilted just a little bit on its axis. And the sun, a giant ball of fire, is our constant dance partner."

Paarth's eyes widened. "A dance? But the sun is so big, and the Earth is just a tiny ball!"

Their father chuckled. "You're right, Paarth. The sun is much bigger, but even the smallest tilt can have a big impact. As the Earth twirls around the sun, different parts get to be closer to the sun at different times, like spotlight dancers on a giant stage."

Aarika's face lit up. "So, when we're closer to the sun, it's like being in the spotlight? That's why it's hot and sunny then?"

Their father smiled. "Exactly, Aarika! The closer we are to the sun, the more sunlight we receive, making it warm and sunny – that's summer. But as the Earth keeps spinning, we slowly tilt away from the sun, like a dancer stepping out of the spotlight."

He gestured towards the window. "See how the sunlight seems to slant lower across the sky now, even though it's still summer? That's because we're starting to tilt away a little bit."

Paarth, finally understanding, bounced with excitement. "So, when we're all the way turned away, that's winter? No more spotlight, so we get cold and snowy?"

Their father ruffled his hair playfully. "Not quite all the way turned away, Paarth, but close enough! Winter brings less sunlight, making things colder. And in between these two extremes, spring and autumn come to play, like the stage hands setting up for the next act in the grand cosmic dance."

Aarika and Paarth sat in comfortable silence, the vastness of space and the Earth's grand dance swirling in their imaginations. The changing seasons weren't just about hot and cold anymore; they were a story written across the sky, a story of movement, light, and the delicate balance that sustained their world.

"So, it's like the Earth is strolling with the sun?" Aarika finally whispered, her voice filled with awe.

Their father smiled, his heart swelling with their wonder. "Exactly, Aarika. And we, along with everything else on Earth, get to be a part of this beautiful, never-ending dance."

From that day on, Aarika and Paarth looked at the changing seasons with new eyes. They saw the Earth's tilt not as a random occurrence, but as a graceful movement in a cosmic ballet, a constant reminder of the delicate balance that allowed life to flourish on their tiny blue planet.

■■■

CHAPTER 14

WHAT MAKES THE MOON SHINE?

A blanket of twilight had draped itself over the world, painting the sky in hues of orange and purple. Aarika and Paarth, nestled on the living room rug, gazed out the window with wide eyes. The moon, a luminous pearl in the darkening sky, seemed to hold a silent conversation with them, its gentle glow sparking a question in Paarth's mind.

"Papa," he began, his voice hushed with a reverence that mirrored the moonlit scene, "What makes the moon shine? Is it a giant nightlight someone forgot to turn off?"

Aarika giggled at the image, but her own curiosity burned bright. "Maybe it has its own special light switch, hidden on the dark side we can't see?"

Their father smiled, the sound warm and inviting in the twilight hush. He settled down beside them, his presence a comforting anchor in the vastness of the night sky.

"Those are both very creative ideas," he admitted, his eyes twinkling like distant stars. "But the truth about the moon's light is a little different. It's not a nightlight, nor does it have a hidden switch."

Paarth's eyebrows creased in with focus. "Then how does it shine so brightly? It lights up our whole room sometimes!"

Aarika, ever the dreamer, reached out a hand as if to touch the moon's luminous face. "Maybe it captures sunlight during the day and stores it for night time, like a giant glow-in-the-dark sticker!"

Their father smiled, his heart overflowing with their innocent wonder. "Not quite like a glow-in-the-dark sticker, Aarika," he explained, "but the idea of capturing light is on the right track."

He pointed towards the moon, its cratered surface stark against the inky black sky. "The moon itself doesn't actually make its own light. It's more like a giant mirror, floating in the vast darkness."

Paarth's eyes widened. "A mirror? But how can a mirror shine in the dark?"

"A very good question, Paarth," their father said, pulling them both into a hug. "The answer lies with our giant, glowing friend – the sun."

He gestured towards the horizon, where the last sliver of sunlight was fading. "Imagine the sun as a giant lamp, shining its light across the universe. And the moon, our celestial mirror, catches some of that sunlight and reflects it back towards us."

Aarika's face lit up with understanding. "So, when we see the moon shining, it's really just borrowed light from the sun?"

Their father nodded. "Exactly, Aarika! The moon itself is dark, but it reflects the sun's light, making it appear bright and beautiful in the night sky."

Paarth, ever the pragmatist, tilted his head. "But why can't we see the borrowed light all the time? Sometimes the moon is just a sliver, or even completely invisible."

"That's because of how the moon dances around the Earth, Paarth," their father explained. "Just like a mirror held at different angles, the moon reflects sunlight differently depending on its position. Sometimes, it reflects a lot of light, appearing big and bright. Other times, only a small part of the moon faces the sun, so we see a crescent moon or no moon at all."

Aarika and Paarth sat in comfortable silence, the vastness of space and the moon's celestial dance swirling in their imaginations. The moon wasn't just a glowing orb anymore; it was a cosmic mirror, a silent storyteller reflecting the sun's light and whispering tales of celestial journeys.

"So, the moon is like a secret sharer of the sun's light?" Aarika finally whispered; her voice filled with awe.

Their father smiled, his heart swelling with their wonder. "Yes, Aarika," he said. "The moon, a borrowed light in the vast darkness, a silent reminder of the interconnectedness of everything in the universe."

From that night on, Aarika and Paarth looked at the moon with new eyes. They saw it not just as a source of night time light, but as a celestial bridge, a silent dancer reflecting the sun's brilliance and reminding them of the beautiful stories whispered by the cosmos.

■■■

CHAPTER 15

WHY DO WE CELEBRATE FESTIVALS?

The air crackled with an electric anticipation. Strings of colourful lights twinkled like captured stars, and the aroma of frying sweets filled the crisp winter air. Aarika and Paarth bounced on the balls of their feet, their eyes wide with excitement as they watched their parents string marigolds, their vibrant orange a stark contrast to the vibrant red and green of the approaching Diwali celebration.

"Papa," Aarika finally burst out, her voice barely containing her excitement, "Why do we celebrate Diwali? Is it because it's the brightest night of the year?"

Paarth, always the practical among the duo, enquired, "Yeah, and why do we light Diyas and wear new clothes? Is it to scare away the darkness?"

Their father giggled, a warm sound that mingled with the festive energy swirling around them. He knelt before them, his eyes twinkling with the same joyful anticipation that filled theirs.

"Well, Aarika," he began, his voice gentle, "Diwali is much more than just the brightest night of the year. It's a celebration of light, a time to chase away darkness, not just from our homes, but from our hearts and minds."

Aarika's brow furrowed. "Darkness in our hearts? But why would we have darkness in our hearts?"

Their father pulled her close, his touch a warm reassurance. "Sometimes, Aarika, we all experience little bits of darkness – sadness, anger, or fear. But Diwali reminds us that even in the darkest night, light can always triumph."

He gestured towards the strings of lights. "See how they chase away the shadows? The diyas we light are like tiny flames of hope, reminding us of the good in the world and the strength we have within ourselves."

Paarth, still curious, tugged on his father's sleeve. “But what about the new clothes and sweets? Are those to celebrate the light winning?”

Aarika's eyes sparkled. “Maybe the sweets are like little bursts of happiness, and the new clothes are like wearing our hope on our sleeves!”

Their father laughed, a sound as rich and sweet as the promised Diwali treats. “Not quite like wearing hope on your sleeves, Aarika, but close! The new clothes symbolize new beginnings, a chance to start fresh and embrace the light within us.”

He looked at them both, his gaze filled with love and pride. “But most importantly, Aarika and Paarth, Diwali is a celebration of family and community. It's a time to come together, share stories, laughter, and delicious food. It's a reminder that even though we may face darkness sometimes, together, we can always find the light.”

Their father asked, “Do you know, how did this festival begin?”

“Yes”, Aarika popped in.

“Mumma, has told us the legend behind Diwali. It is celebrated as a homecoming of Shree Prabhu Ram ji to Ayodhya, his home. In the famous victory of good over evil when he with his Vaanar Sena (Army of Monkey Men) defeated Ravan, and brought back Shree Sita Ji Mata, the entire Ayodhya Nagri celebrated by decorating their homes with diyas and cracking firecrackers. Since then, we have been celebrating Diwali”

“And Mumma say's it's been more than 10,000 years now”added Paarth with his piece of extra information.

“Wow, that's real deep knowledge that you have about this grand festival of Hindus. Just that I would like add we do so every year so that we can spread the spirit of brotherhood, love, and positivity on this day,” said their father.

And then as the night deepened, and the diyas cast their warm glow on their faces, Aarika and Paarth understood that Diwali wasn't just about lights and sweets. It was a celebration woven from the threads of their heritage, a reminder that joy, hope, and togetherness were the truest forms of light, capable of chasing away any darkness that might lurk within or around them.

The following day, dressed in their new clothes, they walked hand-in-hand with their parents, sharing sweets with friends and neighbours. The air thrummed with laughter and music, a vibrant tapestry of community and joy. In their hearts, a new understanding bloomed – Diwali wasn't just a festival; it was a promise, a promise to carry the light of hope, gratitude, and togetherness throughout the year, a reminder that even the smallest flame could illuminate the world.

■■■

CHAPTER 16

WHY DO PEOPLE HAVE DIFFERENT SKIN COLOURS?

Aarika gazed at her reflection in the window, her forehead creased in deep thought. The afternoon sun cast a warm glow on their living room, highlighting her rich brown skin and the wild mess of her black curls. A question, whispered amongst kids at school, bloomed in her mind, a seed of curiosity demanding to be planted.

"Papa," she began, her voice barely above a whisper, "Why are some people brown like me, and others are pink or white?"

Paarth, sprawled on the floor with his toy trucks, glanced up, his brow mirroring her confusion. "Yeah, it's like everyone has a different paint colour for their skin!"

Their father, ever the patient listener, looked up from his book, a warm smile gracing his lips. He pulled them both into a hug, the familiar scent of his cologne a comforting presence.

"A very interesting question, Aarika," he said, his voice gentle. "The colour of our skin, like the stripes on a zebra or the spots on a ladybug, is a special story written in our genes, passed down from our families for generations."

Aarika's eyes widened. "A story in our genes? Like a secret code?"

Their father chuckled. "Not exactly a secret code, Aarika, but more like a special instruction manual. One of the instructions tells our bodies how much melanin to produce."

He pulled out a colourful picture book filled with images of children from all over the world, their skin tones a vibrant tapestry of humanity.

"Melanin," he explained, pointing to a picture of a child with dark skin playing on a sunny beach," is like a natural sunscreen our bodies make. The more melanin we have, the darker our skin appears, and the better protected we are from the sun's strong rays."

Paarth's eyes sparkled with understanding. "So, people who live in really sunny places, like on the beach in that picture, need more sunscreen built-in?"

Their father nodded. "Exactly, Paarth. People from places with a lot of sunshine, like Africa or India, tend to have more melanin in their skin, making it darker. This helps protect them from getting sunburned."

He flipped the page to a picture of children playing in a snowy landscape."On the other hand, people who live in places with less sunlight, like Scandinavia or some parts of Asia, have less melanin in their skin, making it appear lighter. This allows them to absorb more sunlight, which is important for getting vitamin D."

Aarika traced the picture of the children playing in the snow, a new appreciation blooming in her heart. "So, our skin colour isn't just about how we look, it's about how our bodies protect themselves from the sun?"

Their father smiled, his heart swelling with pride. "Exactly, Aarika! The different colours of our skin are like superpowers, helping us thrive in the places where our families have lived for generations."

"But then papa why is Paarth fairer than me?" asked Aarika.

Their father knew this was coming soon. He said, "I am sure you know me and your Mum'ma come from two different parts of the country genetically; I am from Kerala and your mother from Uttar Pradesh," their father explained. "That's why you two have such different skin colours—one very fair and the other comparatively brown. It's just the beauty of genetic diversity at work."

"Genetic Diversity?" what in the world does that mean? asked Paarth.

"Genetic diversity," their father said with a smile," means the variety in our genes, which makes everyone unique. It's why you and your sister look different even though you're twins. It's like mixing different paints to create new colours."

"Jeans? But that's something we wear. What's that got to do with our skin colour?" Aarika asked innocently.

Their father smiled at her innocence and said, "No, not jeans you wear, Aarika. I mean genes—G-E-N-E-S. They are the building blocks that determine how we look, like our skin colour, hair, and eyes. And because your mum'ma and I come from different parts of the country, your genes combined to create unique looks for each of you. Pretty cool, right?"

"Ohhh, I get it now! So, it's like a magic recipe that make s me and Aarika different and special," Paarth said, giggling.

They all started laughing out loud.

The father looked at both of them, his gaze filled with love. "Remember, Aarika and Paarth, skin colour doesn't define who you are. It's just one part of the beautiful story you carry within you, a story woven from your heritage and passed down through time."

From that day on, Aarika and Paarth saw the world with new eyes. The different skin tones they encountered weren't just colours; they were stories whispered on the breeze, tales of resilience, adaptation, and the beautiful tapestry of humanity woven together under the same sun. They learned to celebrate their own unique colours, while cherishing the vibrant stories written on the skin of everyone they met. Their world became a richer, more vibrant place, a canvas splashed with the colours of acceptance, understanding, and the knowledge that beneath the surface, we were all connected by the invisible threads of our shared humanity.

■■■

CHAPTER 17:
HOW DO PLANTS GROW?

Aarika skipped alongside her father, her ponytail bouncing with each step. They were on their way to the community garden, a vibrant haven buzzing with life. Sunlight dappled through the leaves, casting playful patterns on the ground, and the air hummed with the contented drone of bees. But amidst the joyful chaos, a question bloomed in Aarika's mind.

"Papa," she began, her voice filled with wonder as she stopped to admire a plump tomato ripening on the vine, "How do these plants grow so big and strong? Do they have a secret recipe?"

Paarth, ever the practical one, added, "Yeah, and why do they need all that dirt? Can't they just eat cookies like us?"

Their father smiled, the sound warm and inviting like the sunshine filtering through the leaves. He knelt before them, his weathered hands brushing the soft earth.

"Growing isn't quite like baking cookies, Paarth," he explained, his voice gentle. "But plants do have their own secret recipe, a recipe for life written in the language of nature."

Aarika's eyes widened. "A secret recipe written in nature? Can we learn it?"

Their father smiled. "Of course you can, Aarika! The first ingredient is sunshine." He pointed towards a sunflower, its golden face basking in the sun's warmth.

"See how the sunflower stretches its face towards the sun? Plants use sunlight like a magic ingredient, a power source to make their own food through a process called photosynthesis."

Paarth scrunched up his nose. "Photosynthesis? Sounds complicated."

Their father ruffled his hair playfully. “Not as complicated as it sounds, Paarth. Imagine sunlight as tiny golden coins, and the plant's leaves as little factories.”

He held up a leaf, its intricate veins shining in the sunlight. “These factories use the sunlight coins, along with another ingredient – water – to cook up their special food.”

He gestured towards a hosepipe snaking through the garden, its spray glistening like tiny diamonds. “Plants slurp up water through their roots, like tiny straws, and transport it up to their leaves.”

Aarika's face lit up with understanding. “So, the water helps them mix the sunlight coins and make their food?”

Their father nodded, his eyes twinkling with pride at her growing understanding. “Exactly, Aarika! But that's not all. They also need a little bit of air, which they take in through tiny pores on their leaves, and some nutrients from the soil, which their roots gobble up.”

He carefully dug up a handful of moist earth, revealing a network of tiny white roots. “These roots act like busy chefs, searching the soil for the vitamins and minerals the plants need to grow big and strong.”

Aarika stared at the roots with newfound respect. “So, it's like teamwork? The sunshine, water, air, and soil all work together to help the plants grow?”

Their father smiled, pulling them both into a hug. “Exactly, Aarika! Plants are like little magicians, using the power of nature to transform simple ingredients into life itself.”

As they continued their walk through the garden, Aarika and Paarth no longer saw just rows of vegetables and flowers. They saw living stories unfolding, testaments to the magic of nature's recipe. They learned that growth wasn't just about getting bigger, but about a remarkable collaboration between sunshine, water, air, and earth, a silent symphony that nurtured life in all its vibrant forms.

From that day on, Aarika and Paarth looked at plants with a newfound appreciation. They understood the silent language of photosynthesis, the dance between roots and soil, and the invisible threads that connected all living things under the sun. The garden became more than just a place to play; it became a classroom filled with the secrets of life, a reminder that even the smallest seed held the potential for extraordinary growth.

■■■

CHAPTER 18

WHY DO WE HAVE TO EAT VEGETABLES?

Aarika stared at her plate, a fortress of green beans with a few pieces of potatoes. Her nose wrinkled, and a dramatic sigh escaped her lips.

"Mumma," she announced, her voice heavy with mock despair, "These greens again? Can't we have something more...exciting for dinner?"

Paarth, who always had something to add, said"Yeah, why can't we just have pizza every night? It's like fireworks in your mouth!"

Their father who was helping their mother in the kitchen giggled, the sound warm and familiar. He pulled up a chair, his presence a comforting anchor at the dinner table.

"Pizza is delicious, Paarth," he admitted, his eyes twinkling, "But vegetables are like tiny superheroes for your body. They might not be as flashy as pizza, but they have hidden powers that keep you healthy and strong."

Aarika's eyes widened. "Hidden powers? Like what?"

Their father reached into his pocket and pulled out a stack of colourful cards. On each card was a picture of a different vegetable, a vibrant superhero in its own right.

"See this one?" he asked, holding up a card with a picture of a bright orange carrot. "This is Captain Carotene, rich in vitamin A, which helps you see clearly, especially at night, almost like having supervision!"

Aarika gasped, her imagination ignited. "Wow! So, carrots can help me see in the dark?"

Their father winked. "Not exactly see in the dark, Aarika, but they do help keep your eyes healthy. And this one," he continued, holding up a card with a picture of a leafy green spinach, "Is Iron Man Spinach! It's loaded with iron, which helps carry oxygen throughout your body, giving you the energy to run and play all day long."

Paarth's eyes sparkled with newfound interest. "So, spinach gives you super speed?"

Their father chuckled. "Not quite super speed, Paarth, but it does help your body feel energized and ready for adventures."

He flipped through the cards, each vegetable a champion with its own unique power. Broccoli for strong bones, like a tiny bone shield. Bell peppers for a healthy immune system, acting as a personal bodyguard against sickness. Every vegetable held a secret waiting to be unlocked.

Aarika picked up the broccoli floret on her plate with newfound respect. "So, even though they might not look exciting, these broccoli trees are like tiny shields protecting me from getting sick?"

Their father smiled, his heart swelling with pride. "Exactly, Aarika! Vegetables may not be as flashy as pizza, but they are packed with essential nutrients that help your body grow strong, fight off illness, and give you the energy to explore the world."

He took a bite of his vegetables, savoring the flavor. "Besides," he added with a wink, "Sometimes, even superheroes need to eat their greens to keep their powers strong."

Aarika and Paarth looked at their plates with a newfound appreciation. The vegetables were no longer just food; they were tiny powerhouses, each bite a step towards becoming stronger, healthier versions of themselves. With a newfound determination, they began their meal, ready to unlock the hidden potential within each bite. Dinner wasn't just a meal anymore; it was a training ground for future adventures, fueled by the extraordinary power of vegetables.

CHAPTER 19

HOW DO FISH BREATHE UNDERWATER?

Aarika and Paarth pressed their noses against the cool glass of the aquarium, their faces alight with wonder. Inside, a kaleidoscope of colours danced – shimmering scales, flowing fins, and eyes that reflected the light like tiny jewels. But amidst the captivating scene, a question bubbled up in Paarth's mind, a wrinkle appearing on his eyebrow.

"Papa," he began, his voice barely above a whisper, "How do these fishies breathe down there? Don't they need air, like us?"

Aarika, always the observer, looked up, her eyes wide with curiosity. "Yeah, they don't have noses! Do they just hold their breath all the time?"

Their father smiled, the sound warm and inviting. He knelt beside them, his presence a comforting anchor in the sea of vibrant fish.

"Those are great questions, Aarika and Paarth," he said, his voice gentle. "While we breathe air with our lungs, fish have a different, but equally amazing, way of getting the oxygen they need."

He pointed towards a goldfish with sparkling scales, its gills flaring rhythmically on either side of its head.

"See those feathery things behind their fins? Those are their gills, like special underwater lungs."

Aarika's eyes widened. "Underwater lungs? That sounds like something out of a mermaid story!"

Their father smiled. "Not quite a mermaid story, Aarika, but just as fascinating. Gills are covered in tiny blood vessels, and as water passes over them, the oxygen in the water dissolves and gets absorbed into the fish's bloodstream."

Paarth scrunched up his nose in concentration. "So, the water has oxygen in it, even though we can't see it?"

Their father nodded. "Exactly, Paarth! The water holds dissolved oxygen, just like air does, but in a much smaller amount. That's why fish have these specially designed gills to extract it efficiently."

He pointed towards a bubble stream rising from the bottom of the tank. "See those bubbles? That's the carbon dioxide the fish breathe out, similar to how we release it when we exhale."

Aarika traced the path of the bubbles with her finger, a sense of awe blooming in her chest. "So, it's like a trade? They take the oxygen the water has hidden and give back something else?"

Their father smiled, his heart swelling with pride at their growing understanding. "Exactly, Aarika! It's a beautiful exchange, a cycle that keeps the underwater world alive."

They spent the rest of the afternoon lost in the mesmerizing world of the aquarium. Each fish they saw became a testament to the wonders of adaptation, a silent story of survival in a world so different from their own. They learned that gills weren't just organs; they were badges of courage, allowing fish to thrive in the cool depths, forever connected to the water that cradled their lives.

From that day on, Aarika and Paarth looked at any body of water with a newfound respect. It wasn't just a pond or a stream; it was a hidden world teeming with life, a silent testament to the remarkable ways nature had equipped its creatures to breathe, to survive, and to paint the underwater world with vibrant colours and fascinating stories.

■■■

CHAPTER 20

WHY DO WE HAVE TO SLEEP?

A wave of exhaustion washed over Aarika, her eyelids drooping like tired butterflies. She stifled a yawn, her body yearning for the comfort of her bed. But curiosity, a persistent itch in her mind, wouldn't let her surrender to sleep just yet.

"Papa," she mumbled, her voice thick with sleepiness, "Why do we have to go to bed every night? Can't we just stay up and play all the time?"

Paarth, usually wide-eyed and energetic, mirrored her weariness. He slumped against their father, his voice barely a whisper. "Yeah, sleep seems like a waste of time. Can't we just explore the world 24/7?"

Their father chuckled, the sound warm and comforting in the lamplit room. He pulled them both into a hug, his touch a familiar anchor in the sea of drowsiness.

"Sleep might seem boring, Aarika and Paarth," he admitted, his voice gentle, "but it's actually a secret superpower our bodies have."

Aarika's eyes fluttered open, a spark of curiosity reignited. "A superpower? What kind of superpower?"

Their father smiled. "Think of sleep as a magic night spa for your body and brain. While you're snuggled under the covers, amazing things are happening inside you."

He pointed to Aarika's head. "Your brain is like a busy beehive during the day, buzzing with thoughts, memories, and everything you learn and experience. But at night, during sleep, it gets a chance to clean up and sort through all that information, filing it away neatly for future use."

Paarth's brow furrowed. "So, sleep is like tidying up our brains?"

Their father nodded. "Exactly, Paarth! But that's not all. Sleep is also like a magic repair shop for your body. Just like your favourite toy car needs a break sometimes, your body uses sleep to mend tired muscles and grow strong for the next day's adventures."

Aarika snuggled closer, a sense of wonder replacing her initial resistance. "So, when we sleep, our bodies are secretly becoming stronger?"

Their father smiled. "Absolutely, Aarika! Sleep is like a magic syrup that helps you grow taller, fight off sickness, and wake up feeling refreshed and ready to take on the day."

He looked at both of them, his gaze filled with love. "Remember, Aarika and Paarth, sleep isn't a punishment; it's a gift. It's a time for your body and brain to recharge and get ready for all the amazing things tomorrow brings."

With a newfound appreciation for sleep's hidden power, Aarika and Paarth drifted off, their dreams filled with fantastical adventures fueled by a night of growth, repair, and magical brain-tidying. They no longer saw sleep as the end of the day, but as the beginning of a nightly transformation, a secret superpower that prepared them to face the world, well-rested and ready to explore.

■■■

CHAPTER 21

WHY DO I HAVE TO BRUSH MY TEETH EVERY DAY?

Paarth scrunched up his nose, his face contorted in disgust. He pointed a grubby finger towards Aarika, who was giggling uncontrollably.

"Eww, Aarika!" he shrieked, "Your breath smells like yesterday's school socks!"

Aarika stuck her tongue out, but a seed of doubt bloomed in her chest. Was her breath really that bad? A worried frown settled on her face.

Later that evening, as they prepared for bed, Aarika hesitantly approached their father, her voice barely above a whisper. "Papa," she began, "Does my breath really smell bad?"

Paarth jumped in, his voice laced with a hint of fear, "And what happens if we don't brush our teeth? Do they just fall out and become tooth fairies?"

Their father smiled, the sound warm and inviting. He pulled them both into a hug, his touch a familiar comfort.

"Well, Aarika and Paarth," he began, his voice gentle, "Our mouths are like busy playgrounds for tiny creatures called bacteria."

Aarika's eyes widened. "Bacteria? Like the ones that make us sick?"

Their father nodded. "There are good and bad bacteria in our mouths, Aarika. The good ones help us digest food, but the bad ones love to munch on leftover sugar and food particles."

He made a face. "And when these bad bacteria have a sugary feast, they leave behind a sticky mess that can make your breath smell not so-fresh, kind of like a forgotten school sock left under your bed, Paarth."

Paarth's eyes widened in horror, and Aarika scrunched up her nose in disgust. The image was vivid, and the realization hit them like a wave.

"So, brushing our teeth is like giving our mouths a bath?" Aarika asked, a sliver of understanding peeking through.

Their father smiled. "Exactly, Aarika! Brushing your teeth twice a day, in the morning and before bed, is like giving those bad bacteria the boot. It washes away the leftover food they like to munch on, keeping your mouth clean and your breath fresh."

Paarth's fear morphed into determination. "So, if we brush well, the tooth fairy won't need to collect our teeth early?"

Their father laughed. "Exactly, Paarth! Brushing keeps your teeth strong and healthy, so they can last a lifetime of chewing delicious food and smiling wide."

He grabbed their toothbrushes, their colourful handles glinting in the lamplight. "Think of your toothbrushes as tiny superhero tools! They fight off the bad bacteria and keep your mouth healthy and happy."

From that day on, brushing teeth became an adventure. Aarika and Paarth wielded their toothbrushes with newfound purpose, vanquishing the sugar-loving bacteria and keeping their smiles sparkling. Brushing wasn't just a chore anymore; it was a quest for a healthy mouth, a battle against invisible enemies, and a celebration of fresh breath and strong teeth that would last a lifetime of adventures.

■■■

CHAPTER 22

WHY DO I FEEL SCARED SOMETIMES?

A tear trembled on Aarika's cheek, threatening to spill over. Her lower lip quivered, and her normally bright eyes were clouded with fear. A monstrous thunderstorm raged outside, the wind howling like a wounded beast, and each flash of lightning illuminated the room with an eerie glow.

"Papa," she whimpered, her voice barely audible over the roar of the storm, "What if the lightning hits our house? What if the monsters in my closet come alive?"

Paarth, usually fearless, inched closer to their father, his own eyes wide with apprehension. "Yeah, and what if the thunder is a giant angry voice yelling at us?"

Their father pulled them both into a warm embrace, a comforting shield against the storm's fury. He knelt before them, his gaze filled with understanding and love.

"Feeling scared during a storm is perfectly normal, Aarika," he said, his voice a soothing balm. "It's your body's way of saying, Hey, be careful! Something big and loud is happening!"

Aarika sniffled, wiping her nose on her sleeve. "So, my body is just trying to protect me?"

Their father nodded. "Exactly, Aarika! It's like having a tiny bodyguard inside you, always looking out for your safety. Sometimes, that bodyguard can be a little overprotective, like when there are no real monsters in your closet, just friendly pajamas."

He chuckled, a warm sound that calmed the storm within them. "But it's okay to feel scared sometimes, even if there's nothing to be scared of. Sometimes, our imaginations can play tricks on us, making shadows seem like monsters and loud noises seem like angry voices."

Paarth, his fear subsiding, looked out the window at the lightning, now a source of fascination. "So, the thunder isn't a giant voice yelling at us? It's just...electricity in the sky?"

Their father smiled. "Exactly, Paarth! Sometimes, understanding what something is can help us feel less scared of it. Lightning is like a tiny spark, like the one that makes the light bulb in your room turn on, only much bigger and way up in the sky."

He looked at both of them, his gaze filled with love. "Remember, Aarika and Paarth, it's okay to feel scared sometimes. And you know what? The bravest people aren't those who never feel scared, but those who face their fears and know they can talk about them. We're always here to listen, hold your hand, and help you chase away any scary shadows, real or imagined."

With a newfound understanding, Aarika and Paarth snuggled closer to their father. The storm outside continued its rampage, but within their embrace, they felt safe and loved. They learned that fear wasn't a monster to be banished, but a signal to be understood. And with their father by their side, they knew they could face any storm, real or imagined, hand-in-hand, hearts full of courage and love.

■■■

CHAPTER 23

WHY DO PEOPLE GET SICK?

A wave of nausea washed over Aarika, her stomach churning like a stormy sea. Her head throbbed with a dull ache, and each cough felt like a tiny explosion in her chest. Tears welled up in her eyes, blurring the world around her.

"Papa," she whimpered, her voice weak and raspy, "Why do I feel so awful?"

Paarth, usually brimming with energy, sat beside her on the couch, his eyebrows furrowed with concern. "Yeah, it's like there's a tiny monster living inside you, making you all achy and grumpy!"

Their father placed a cool hand on Aarika's forehead, his touch a comforting anchor in her sea of misery. He pulled them both into a hug, his familiar scent a balm against the rising tide of fear.

"Sometimes, Aarika and Paarth," he began, his voice gentle, "Our bodies get invaded by tiny, invisible enemies called germs."

Aarika's eyes widened. "Invisible enemies? Like the villains in my comic books?"

Their father chuckled a warm sound that soothed her a little. "Not quite like villains, Aarika, but these germs can make us feel pretty crummy. They can be like viruses or bacteria, so small you can't even see them, but they can multiply really fast and make us feel sick."

Paarth crunched up his nose in disgust. "So, these germs are like icky spies sneaking into our bodies to make us miserable?"

Their father nodded. "In a way, Paarth. But luckily, our bodies have amazing defenses, like a mighty army called the immune system."

He held up a fist, his voice strong. "The immune system is full of tiny warriors – white blood cells and antibodies – that fight off these germs and keep us healthy. They're like superheroes patrolling our bodies, always on the lookout for trouble."

Aarika, captivated by the image, whispered, "So, my body is having a superhero battle inside right now?"

Their father smiled. "Exactly, Aarika! But sometimes, the germs can be extra strong or sneaky, and they overpower the good guys for a little while. That's when we feel sick, with headaches, coughs, and feeling achy all over."

He squeezed their hands gently. "But don't worry! There are things we can do to help our immune system stay strong. We can eat healthy foods to give our superhero warriors the energy they need to fight. We can get enough sleep so they can rest and recharge. And washing our hands regularly helps keep those icky germs away from our bodies in the first place."

Paarth's eyes shone with determination. "So, it's like giving our immune system a big power-up to fight the bad guys?"

Their father ruffled his hair playfully. "Exactly, Paarth! And if the germs do win a small battle, don't worry. We have doctors, like real-life superheroes with stethoscopes and medicines, who can help us get better faster."

Aarika, feeling a sliver of hope bloom in her chest, leaned against her father. The battle within her body might be raging, but with her immune system's brave warriors and the love of her family, she knew she would win the war. Feeling sick wasn't fun, but it was a reminder of the incredible battle happening within her, a testament to the strength of her body and the power of love that helped her heal.

From that day on, Aarika and Paarth saw their bodies not just as vessels, but as fortresses to be protected, fueled by healthy habits and cheered on by the unwavering love of their family. The fight against germs became a shared mission, a testament to the resilience of the human body and the invisible superheroes that kept them healthy and strong.

■■■

CHAPTER 24

WHY CAN'T I EAT CANDY ALL THE TIME?

A tear welled up in Aarika's eye, threatening to spill over like a waterfall of disappointment. Her gaze lingered longingly on the jar of colourful candies on the counter, each one a sugary promise of pure joy.

"Papa," she whimpered, her voice heavy with childish heartbreak, "Why can't I have just one more? They're like tiny rainbows in my mouth!"

Paarth, usually a whirlwind of energy, mirrored her dejection. He slumped against their father, his lower lip trembling. "Yeah, can't we just pretend it's our birthday every day and have cake for every meal?"

Their father crouched before them, his presence a comforting anchor in the sea of sugary cravings. He gently placed a hand on Aarika's head, his touch a silent promise of understanding.

"Candy is delicious, Aarika, I won't deny that," he admitted, his voice laced with empathy. "Those bright colours and sweet flavors can be like a party in your mouth."

A glimmer of hope sparked in Aarika's eyes. "So, why can't we have a party every day?"

Their father smiled, a hint of sadness flickering in his eyes. "Because, Aarika, just like a party that never ends gets boring, too much candy isn't good for your body. It's like giving your body a whole bunch of sugar fireworks, but without the real celebration."

Paarth's brow furrowed in concentration. "So, the candy makes my body feel tired instead of excited?"

Their father nodded. "Exactly, Paarth. Candy has a lot of sugar, and while it gives you a quick burst of energy, it doesn't have the vitamins and nutrients your body needs to grow strong and healthy. It's like giving your car a tank full of candy instead of real fuel – it might run for a bit, but it won't get you very far."

Aarika's eyes widened. "So, my body needs healthy food to be like a strong, fast car?"

Their father's smile broadened. "Absolutely, Aarika! Fruits and vegetables are like super fuel for your body. They give you the energy to play all day, help you fight off sickness, and even make your hair shine and your smile sparkle."

He reached into a fruit basket and pulled out a bright red apple. "See this apple? It's like a tiny treasure chest filled with vitamins and healthy sugars that your body can use to build strong bones and muscles."

He handed the apple to Aarika, its smooth skin cool against her hand. "Eating healthy foods most of the time is like taking care of your body, making it a strong and healthy machine that can do amazing things."

Paarth's eyes lit up with a newfound determination. "So, we can still have candy sometimes, like a special reward for being healthy superheroes?"

Their father ruffled Paarth's hair playfully. "Exactly, Paarth! Sweets can be a fun treat, but remember, healthy foods are the real superheroes that keep your body running strong and ready for all your adventures."

From that day on, Aarika and Paarth saw fruits and vegetables not just as boring health food, but as the fuel that powered their bodies. They approached the dinner table with renewed enthusiasm, their taste buds excited for the delicious adventures healthy eating could take them on. Candy remained a sweet treat, a reward for their healthy choices, a reminder of the importance of balance and the power of good nutrition to make them strong, healthy, and ready to conquer any challenge life threw their way.

■■■

CHAPTER 25

WHAT HAPPENS WHEN YOU DIE?

A lump formed in Aarika's throat, her usually bright eyes filled with a sudden, unfamiliar fear. The question that had swirled unspoken in her mind for weeks finally tumbled out, a whisper barely audible.

"Papa," she began, her voice trembling, "What happens when we…die?"

The room seemed to grow quiet, the air heavy with unspoken emotions. Paarth, who had been engrossed in a sketching his famous Naruto, looked up, his playful smile replaced by a mirroring worry.

Their father knelt before them, his gaze filled with a gentle understanding. He pulled them both into a warm embrace, a comforting shield against the tide of fear that threatened to engulf them.

"That's a very big question, Aarika," he said, his voice soft and reassuring. "It's something that people have wondered about for as long as there have been stories."

Aarika sniffled, her small hand clutching her father's shirt. "Is it like falling asleep, but forever?"

Her father shook his head. "Not quite like sleep, Aarika. It's more like the end of a long journey. Our bodies get tired, just like after a long adventure."

Paarth, his eyebrows furrowed, chipped in, "But what happens to our minds? Do all our thoughts and memories disappear?"

Their father sighed, a hint of sadness flickering in his eyes. "That's something we don't know for sure, Paarth. Some people believe in a place called heaven, where good people go to be happy after they die."

He looked at Aarika, his gaze filled with love. "Others believe that our energy comes back to earth in a different form, maybe even a tiny baby."

Aarika's eyes widened. "So, I could come back as a fluffy kitten?"

A soft chuckle escaped her father's lips. "Maybe, Aarika. Or a playful puppy, or a beautiful butterfly. The possibilities are endless."

He squeezed their hands gently. "But no matter what people believe, there's one thing that's important – living a good life."

He looked at them, his voice filled with conviction. "Being kind to others, making happy memories with the people you love, and exploring the world with curiosity – that's what truly matters."

Paarth, his fear replaced by a newfound determination, nodded vigorously. "So, as long as we're good and make people happy, even if we die, a part of us stays behind?"

Their father smiled, his eyes shining with pride. "Exactly, Paarth! The love we share, the kindness we show, the joy we bring – those things never truly die. They live on in the hearts of the people we touch."

He looked at Aarika, his gaze filled with love. "Thinking about death can be scary, Aarika, but it's also a reminder to cherish every moment we have. It reminds us to hug our loved ones tight, to tell them how much they mean to us, and to live each day to the fullest, creating a beautiful story that will inspire others long after we're gone."

From that day on, Aarika and Paarth saw life not as a journey with an unknown ending, but as a precious adventure to be savored. They embraced each day with a newfound zest, their hearts overflowing with love and kindness. They knew that even though life may end, the love they shared and the memories they created would ripple outwards, a testament to the beautiful lives they had lived.

■■■

CHAPTER 26

HOW DOES THE TV WORK?

Aarika and Paarth plopped themselves down on the living room rug, their eyes glued to the swirling colours on the TV screen. A cartoon spaceship whooshed across a galaxy far, far away, its adventures captivating their imaginations. But amidst the fantastical scenes, a spark of curiosity ignited in Paarth's mind.

"Papa," he interrupted, his voice filled with wonder, "How does this magic box show us all these amazing things?"

Aarika, equally captivated, jumped in, her brow furrowed in concentration. "Yeah, it's like a window to another world! How does it work?"

Their father chuckled, the sound warm and inviting. He turned off the sound on the TV, momentarily silencing the spaceship's journey.

"That's a great question, Aarika and Paarth," he said, his voice filled with a hint of amusement. "This amazing box we call a TV isn't just magic, though it can sometimes feel that way."

He knelt before them, his presence a comforting anchor in their sea of curiosity. "Imagine the TV as a special decoder ring, but instead of secret messages, it decodes invisible signals."

Paarth's eyes widened. "Invisible signals? Like whispers only the TV can hear?"

Their father smiled. "Exactly, Paarth! These signals can come from a tall tower with antennas called a TV station, or they can travel through the air from special satellites."

He pointed towards the cable box tucked away beneath the TV. "Sometimes, the signals come through a cable, like a secret pathway, bringing these whispers directly to your house."

Aarika, her imagination sparked, gasped. "So, the cable is like a secret tunnel for the whispers?"

Their father's smile broadened. "Exactly, Aarika! These whispers carry tiny pieces of information, like the colours that make up the picture and the sounds that make up the music and voices."

He reached out and gently touched the flat screen. "Inside the TV, there's a special screen that can light up in different colours. The TV's decoder ring takes those tiny pieces of information from the whispers and uses them to paint a picture on the screen, one tiny dot at a time."

Paarth's jaw dropped. "So, millions of tiny dots come together to make the pictures we see?"

Their father nodded. "Millions and millions, Paarth! And the decoder ring also takes the sound information and turns it into the voices and music that fill our ears."

He turned the TV back on, the sound of the spaceship whooshing once again. "So, the next time you watch your favourite show, remember, it's not magic, but a clever combination of whispers, decoder rings, and a million tiny dots working together to bring you stories and information from all over the world."

From that day on, Aarika and Paarth saw the TV not just as a source of entertainment, but as a window to the world, a marvel of technology that translated invisible whispers into the sights and sounds that filled their living room. They marveled at the tiny dots dancing on the screen, understanding the invisible dance that brought their favourite shows to life. The TV remained a source of wonder, but now it was a wonder laced with understanding, a testament to human ingenuity and the invisible signals that connected them to the world around them.

■■■

CHAPTER 27

WHY CAN'T I HAVE A PHONE YET?

Aarika's bottom lip trembled, her eyes welling up with a familiar pang of disappointment. Her friends at school all seemed to have these magical devices – phones – portals to a world of games, videos, and constant connection.

"Papa," she whimpered, her voice thick with envy, "Why can't I have a phone like everyone else? It's not fair!"

Paarth, usually brimming with boundless energy, mirrored her dejection. He slumped against the couch, kicking his legs listlessly. "Yeah, it's like being left out of a secret club! We could play games with our friends all the time."

Their father knelt before them, his gaze filled with a comforting warmth. He pulled them both into a hug, a silent promise of understanding.

"Having a phone is a big responsibility, Aarika and Paarth," he began, his voice gentle but firm. "It's like having a powerful little computer in your pocket, and with great power comes great responsibility, just like Spiderman!"

Aarika perked up at the mention of her favourite superhero. "So, a phone is like a tiny Spiderman suit? But with games instead of webs?"

A hint of amusement flickered in their father's eyes. "Not quite like that, Aarika," he chuckled. "A phone can be amazing, but it can also be distracting. It can be like a portal to another world, one that can sometimes take away from the real world around you."

He gestured towards the backyard bathed in the warm glow of the setting sun. "See those beautiful clouds? Or hear the chirping of the crickets? Sometimes, phones can make us miss these simple joys."

Paarth's brow furrowed in thought. "So, a phone can be a fun distraction, but it can also steal our fun?"

Their father nodded. "Exactly, Paarth. Right now, you're both growing and learning so much. You're discovering new things every day, making friends, and exploring the world around you. A phone can sometimes get in the way of that exploration."

He squeezed their hands gently. "But that doesn't mean you won't have a phone someday. When you're a little older and can handle the responsibility, we can talk about it. We'll teach you how to use it wisely, how to balance screen time with real-life adventures."

Aarika, a sliver of hope blooming in her chest, looked up at her father. "So, it's like training to be a phone superhero? Learning how to use its powers for good?"

Their father smiled, his eyes twinkling. "Exactly, Aarika! And in the meantime, you have your imaginations, your friends, and the whole world to explore. There are so many amazing adventures waiting for you, real-life adventures that a phone screen can't replace."

From that day on, Aarika and Paarth saw the world around them with renewed curiosity. They turned their disappointment into a quest, a mission to become responsible phone users in the future. They explored the backyard with the fervor of young explorers, their imaginations weaving tales far grander than any video game. The phone remained a desired object, but it was no longer a symbol of exclusion. It became a goal, a reward for mastering the art of living in the present, a responsibility to be earned, not a right to be demanded. Their journey towards a phone became a journey of self-discovery, a testament to the power of patience, responsibility, and the boundless adventures that awaited them in the real world.

■■■

CHAPTER 28

WHAT DID YOU DO FOR FUN WHEN YOU WERE MY AGE?

"What Did You Do for Fun When You were My Age?", asked Paarth.

A wave of nostalgia washed over their father as Paarth's question hung in the air. He closed his eyes for a moment, transported back to a simpler time, a time etched in the warm glow of childhood memories.

"Fun," he began, his voice laced with a hint of wistfulness, "Fun when I was your age was a whole different adventure, Aarika and Paarth."

Aarika, perched on the edge of the couch, her eyes wide with curiosity, scooted closer. "A different adventure? How different?"

Their father chuckled, a warm sound that filled the room. "Well, imagine a world without the constant buzz of screens, without games that transport you to fantastical worlds at the touch of a button."

Paarth's brow furrowed. "So, what did you do for fun? Did you just...sit around?"

Their father's smile broadened. "Not at all, Paarth! Our fun was fueled by imagination and the great outdoors. We were like explorers in our own backyards, armed with sticks that transformed into mighty swords and cardboard boxes that became spaceships soaring through galaxies."

He gestured towards the window, where the afternoon sun cast long shadows on the grass. "We spent hours playing cricket in that very field, the thwack of the bat against the ball a symphony to our ears. We had epic games of hide-and-seek, the thrill of the chase coursing through our veins."

Aarika, captivated by the image, gasped. "Did you ever get really good at hiding, Papa? Like invisible ninjas?"

Their father's eyes twinkled with amusement. "Invisible ninjas and fearless pirates, Aarika! We were anything our imaginations could conjure. We climbed trees that scraped the sky, built forts out of blankets and pillows, and spent evenings huddled around a flashlight, devouring the adventures hidden within the pages of a book."

Paarth, a hint of longing creeping into his voice, asked, "But didn't you ever get bored, without all the games and videos we have now?"

Their father shook his head. "Boredom was a rare visitor, Paarth. Our days were filled with the thrill of discovery, the joy of simple pleasures. We learned to create our own fun, to find amusement in the rustle of leaves and the chirping of birds."

He looked at them, his gaze filled with a quiet intensity. "Don't get me wrong, video games can be fun. But there's a magic to be found outside, in the fresh air and the endless possibilities that nature offers. It's a magic that can spark creativity, build friendships, and create memories that will last a lifetime."

Aarika, her imagination ignited, bounced on the couch. "So, can we play pirates in the backyard tomorrow? We can build a ship out of the old sheets and search for buried treasure!"

Their father's smile bloomed. "Absolutely, Aarika! And Paarth, you can be the lookout in the crow's nest, keeping a watchful eye for any sea serpents lurking in the sprinkler."

From that day on, Aarika and Paarth looked at their backyard not just as a yard, but as an uncharted territory waiting to be explored. Their father's stories became their guide, a map leading them to adventures fueled by imagination and the simple joys of the natural world. They discovered that while video games offered a world of digital thrills, the real world held a magic all its own, a magic that whispered tales of pirates, ninjas, and explorers waiting to be born in the fertile ground of their imaginations.

The quest for a phone remained, but it was joined by a newfound appreciation for the adventures waiting just outside their door, a testament to the enduring power of childhood imagination and the timeless joy of creating their own fun.

■■■

CHAPTER 29

HOW DO VIDEO GAMES WORK?

Aarika's eyes sparkled with a mixture of awe and confusion. The fantastical worlds she traversed in her favourite video game felt so real, so alive. But her father's words hung in the air, a puzzle waiting to be solved.

"Papa," she began, her voice laced with childlike wonder, "You said video games are made with code? But how? It doesn't seem like code at all, it's like a whole different world!"

Paarth, usually bouncing with energy, mirrored her contemplative mood. He tilted his head, his brow furrowed in concentration. "Yeah, it's like a magic trick! How can lines of code turn into fire-breathing dragons and knights in shining armor?"

Their father smiled, a warm sound that filled the room. He knelt before them, his presence a comforting anchor in their sea of curiosity.

"You're right, Aarika," he admitted, his voice filled with respect for their wonder. "Those fantastical worlds may seem like magic, but behind the scenes, it's a beautiful blend of creativity and technology."

He reached out and gently tugged at a stray strand of Aarika's hair. "Imagine each strand as a single line of code, Aarika. On its own, it might not seem like much, but when hundreds, thousands, even millions of these lines come together, they can create something incredible."

Paarth's eyes widened. "So, the code is like the building blocks of the game world? Like Legos for a digital world?"

Their father's smile broadened. "Exactly, Paarth! But instead of snapping together plastic bricks, these lines of code tell the game what to do, how to move the characters, and how to react to your actions."

He pointed towards the TV screen where a brave knight battled a fire-breathing dragon. “See how the knight jumps and swings his sword? That's the code telling the game what to do when you press the buttons on your controller.”

Aarika, captivated by the connection, gasped. “So, we're like tiny conductors, using the controller to tell the game what music to play?”

Their father chuckled. “Not exactly music, Aarika, but you're on the right track! You're the hero in this digital story, and the code is your guide, making sure your adventure unfolds in exciting and challenging ways.”

He squeezed their hands gently. “Video games take a lot of creativity, Aarika and Paarth. It's like artists painting a world with code, writers crafting a story with choices, and programmers building a stage for it all to come to life.”

From that day on, Aarika and Paarth saw their video games not just as a source of entertainment, but as a testament to human ingenuity. They looked at the characters on the screen with newfound respect, understanding the invisible symphony of code that breathed life into their digital worlds. The act of playing a game became a collaboration, a dance between their actions and the code that responded, a journey through a world meticulously crafted by creative minds. And while the allure of a phone remained, it was now accompanied by a newfound appreciation for the artistry and wonder that video games held, a world built on the power of code, imagination, and the thrill of the digital adventure.

■■■

CHAPTER 30

WHY DO SOME PEOPLE LIVE ON THE STREETS?

A shadow of worry flickered across Aarika's face as she stared out the window, her gaze landing on a figure huddled in a doorway. The question that had swirled unspoken in her mind for days finally tumbled out, a whisper barely audible.

"Papa," she began, her voice trembling slightly, "Why is that person…sleeping on the street?"

The world seemed to grow quiet, the sounds of the busy city muted by the weight of her question. Paarth, engrossed in his piano keys, looked up, his playful smile replaced by a mirroring concern.

Their father crouched before them, his gaze filled with a gentle understanding. He pulled them both into a warm embrace, a silent shield against the confusion and worry clouding their eyes.

"That's a very important question, Aarika," he said, his voice soft and reassuring. "There are many reasons why someone might not have a home."

Aarika sniffled, her small hand clutching the collar of her father's shirt. "Did they lose something? Like a toy?"

Her father's heart ached for her innocence. He shook his head gently. "Not exactly, Aarika. Sometimes, grown-ups face problems that make it hard to keep a home. They might have lost their jobs, or maybe something happened in their family."

He pointed towards a nearby park, where a group of volunteers were handing out warm meals to people in need. "See those people, Aarika? They're trying to help those who don't have a home by giving them food and a kind word."

Paarth, his brow furrowed in concern, added, "So, they're all alone? Don't they have anyone who loves them?"

Their father sighed, a hint of sadness flickering in his eyes. “Sometimes, Paarth. But it's not because no one loves them. It's just that life can be difficult, and sometimes people need a helping hand.”

He looked at them, his gaze filled with a quiet intensity. “The most important thing to remember is that everyone deserves kindness, Aarika and Paarth. Even if someone doesn't have a home, they have a story, they have feelings, and they deserve to be treated with respect.”

Aarika, a sliver of determination blooming in her chest, looked up at her father. “So, we can help them too? Maybe share some of our toys or clothes?”

A warm smile spread across their father's face. “Exactly, Aarika! There are many ways to help. We can donate clothes and food to shelters, or maybe even volunteer our time to help those in need.”

From that day on, Aarika and Paarth saw the world not just as a place of their own experiences, but as a tapestry woven with stories of joy and hardship. They looked at those living on the streets with empathy, understanding that homelessness wasn't a choice, but a harsh reality some faced. The act of giving became more than just sharing toys or clothes; it became a way of showing compassion, of acknowledging the shared humanity that connected them all. And while the allure of a phone and the thrill of video games remained, they were now accompanied by a newfound desire to make the world a kinder place, a testament to the power of empathy, compassion, and the simple act of helping those in need.

■■■

CHAPTER 31
WHAT IS LOVE?

Aarika twirled a strand of hair around her finger, her brow furrowed in a rare moment of contemplation. The question had been brewing in her mind for days, ever so present in the warm hugs and bedtime stories, yet somehow elusive in its definition.

"Papa," she began, her voice barely above a whisper, "What is love?"

The room seemed to hush, the playful banter between her and Paarth fading into the background. Her father looked at her, his gaze filled with a tenderness that always made her feel safe and loved.

He knelt before her, his presence a comforting anchor. "Love, Aarika," he began, his voice laced with a quiet reverence, "is a very special feeling, like a warm glow that fills your heart."

Aarika's eyes widened. "Like the sunshine in the summer?"

Her father chuckled, a warm sound that filled the room. "In a way, Aarika. Love makes you feel happy and safe, just like the sunshine does on a warm day."

He pulled Paarth, who had been listening intently, into the conversation. "Remember the time you got that new puppy, you found in the society Paarth? How excited you were to play with him and take care of him?"

Paarth's face lit up, a wide grin splitting his face. "Yeah, Sparky! I loved playing fetch with him and wanted to cuddle with him at night."

Their father smiled. "That feeling of excitement, that need to care for Sparky – that's a kind of love, Paarth. It's the love we feel for our pets, a bond of loyalty and companionship."

Aarika, her brow still furrowed in concentration, chimed in, "So, is love just about feeling happy?"

Her father shook his head gently. "Not quite, Aarika. Love is also about caring for someone, even when they're not perfect. It's about wanting them to be happy, even if it means putting their needs before your own."

He looked at both of them, his gaze filled with a love so profound it shone in his eyes. "The love we share as a family, Aarika and Paarth, is the strongest kind of love. It's a love that's always there, no matter what. We fight sometimes, we get frustrated, but our love for each other is what keeps us coming back together, stronger than ever."

Paarth, a hint of wonder in his voice, asked, "So, even when you get mad at us, you still love us?"

Their father pulled them both into a tight hug, the warmth of his embrace a silent confirmation. "Always, Paarth. My love for you is like a big, strong tree. It might sway in the wind sometimes, but its roots are deep, and it will always be there for you."

From that day on, Aarika and Paarth saw love not just as a warm feeling, but as a complex tapestry woven with threads of care, trust, and forgiveness. They looked at their family with new appreciation, understanding the unspoken language of love that bound them together. They began to see love in the acts of kindness they witnessed around them, from a big sister sharing her toys to a friend offering a comforting hug. The world seemed a little brighter, a little kinder, as they learned to recognize the countless ways love bloomed and flourished all around them. And while the desires for a phone and the adventures of video games remained, they were now accompanied by a newfound appreciation for the love that filled their lives, a love that was a constant source of strength, comfort, and the unwavering support of their family.

■■■

CHAPTER 32

WHY DO PEOPLE BELIEVE IN DIFFERENT GODS?

Curiosity crackled in the air, a spark ignited by a question that had been brewing in Paarth's mind for days. He bounced on the balls of his feet, barely able to contain his excitement.

"Papa," he blurted out, his voice brimming with wide-eyed wonder, "Why do people pray to different Gods?"

Aarika, usually lost in her world of imagination, paused, her attention snagged by her brother's question. The world seemed to hush, the playful banter of the afternoon fading into the background.

Their father met their gazes, a gentle smile gracing his lips. He knelt before them, his presence a comforting anchor in the sea of their curiosity.

"That's a very big question, Paarth," he began, his voice filled with respect for their developing minds. "People believe in different things for many reasons, like the stories they hear when they're young, the traditions passed down through families, and even the places they grow up."

He gestured towards the window, where the afternoon sun cast long shadows across the backyard. "Imagine a world as vast as that sky, Aarika. Different cultures, like patches of a beautiful quilt, each with its own stories and beliefs about the world and what lies beyond."

Aarika's eyes widened. "So, the Gods are like different patches on the quilt? Do they all live in the same sky?"

A gentle chuckle escaped their father's lips. "Not quite, Aarika. But the belief in something bigger than ourselves, something that offers comfort and guidance, that's a thread that runs through many cultures."

He looked at Paarth, his gaze filled with a quiet intensity. "For some people, it's one God, for others, it might be many.

These beliefs help people find meaning in life, strengthen them during difficult times, and connect them to a community of like-minded people."

Aarika, her brow furrowed in concentration, chimed in, "But can't there be just one right God, Papa? Like in our storybooks?"

Her father shook his head gently. "The world is a much more colourful place, Aarika. There's beauty in the differences, in learning about how others see the world and what they hold dear."

He squeezed their hands gently. "The most important thing is to respect everyone's beliefs, even if you don't understand them. Just like we wouldn't want someone to make fun of the stories we believe in, we should treat others with kindness and understanding."

From that day on, Aarika and Paarth saw the world not as a place of singular truths, but as a vibrant tapestry woven with threads of diverse beliefs. They approached other cultures with a newfound curiosity, eager to learn about the stories that shaped their faith. Playdates became opportunities to exchange stories, and disagreements morphed into respectful discussions about their differing viewpoints. The world seemed a little bigger, a little richer, as they embraced the beauty of a world where different beliefs could coexist, a testament to the power of respect, understanding, and the vast tapestry of human faith.

■■■

CHAPTER 33

WHY DO WE HAVE TO FOLLOW RULES?

Aarika's bottom lip trembled as she kicked her legs against the couch, a frustrated frown ruining her usually cheerful face. “But Papa,” she wailed, her voice thick with defiance, “Why can't I just stay up a little later tonight? It's not fair!”

Paarth, usually brimming with boundless energy, mirrored her frustration. He slumped against the armrest, his shoulders slumped in defeat. “Yeah, rules are boring! Why can't we just do whatever we want?”

Their father, a familiar warmth radiating from his eyes, knelt before them. He gently placed a hand on Aarika's knee, his touch a silent promise of understanding.

“Rules,” he began, his voice laced with a quiet patience, “I know they can seem annoying sometimes, like a pesky fly buzzing around your head.”

Aarika giggled at the image, a momentary break in her frustration.

“But imagine that fly, Aarika,” he continued, his voice taking on a more serious tone, “was a wasp with a nasty sting. Rules, like walls around your house, are there to keep you safe from those stings.”

Paarth’s brow furrowed in concentration. “So, rules are like guards protecting us from bad things?”

Their father smiled. “Exactly, Paarth! Rules at school, for example, keep everyone safe on the playground. They make sure no one gets hurt during games or gets lost while exploring the schoolyard.”

He gestured towards the window, where children played tag in the park across the street, their laughter echoing in the air. “See how they're all having fun within the boundaries of the game? Rules make the game fair and enjoyable for everyone.”

Aarika, a sliver of understanding blooming in her eyes, asked, "So, rules aren't there to stop us from having fun, but to make sure everyone has fun together?"

"Absolutely, Aarika!" Their father beamed. "Rules also help us learn responsibility. Following a bedtime routine, for example, teaches you the importance of getting enough sleep to be your best self at school."

He reached out and ruffled Paarth's hair playfully. "And remember that time you snuck a cookie before dinner and ended up with a tummy ache? Rules about healthy eating are in place to keep you strong and healthy, Paarth."

Paarth grimaced at the memory, a sheepish grin tugging at his lips.

"Rules can feel restrictive," their father admitted, his voice filled with empathy, "but they provide a foundation for a happy and healthy life. They help us navigate the world, teaching us to be considerate of others and responsible for ourselves."

From that day on, Aarika and Paarth saw rules not just as limitations, but as guideposts on their journey. They began to understand that following rules wasn't about blind obedience, but about creating a safe and harmonious world for everyone. They learned to appreciate the rules' structure, the knowledge that certain actions would lead to certain outcomes, and a sense of security in a world that could sometimes feel overwhelming. And while the allure of staying up late and the occasional desire to bend the rules remained, they were now accompanied by a newfound respect for the role rules played in creating a world where everyone could thrive, a testament to the importance of responsibility, empathy, and the invisible framework that held society together.

■■■

CHAPTER 34

WHAT IS THE MEANING OF LIFE?

A hush fell over the room as Paarth's question hung in the air, heavy with the weight of a universe waiting to be understood. "Papa," he began, his voice barely a whisper, "What's the meaning of life?"

Aarika, usually lost in her world of make-believe, looked up, her eyes mirroring the profound curiosity etched on her brother's face. Their father, a familiar warmth radiating from his eyes, met their gaze with a gentle smile, a silent acknowledgment of the profoundness of their question.

He sat down beside them, pulling them both into a hug, the embrace a comforting anchor in the sea of existential questions swirling in their minds. "That's a very big question, Paarth," he began, his voice laced with a quiet reverence. "A question that philosophers and storytellers have pondered for centuries."

He pulled back slightly, his gaze twinkling with a spark of amusement. "There's no single answer, Paarth. Some people believe the meaning of life is to find happiness, to chase joy and laughter wherever it leads."

Aarika's face lit up, a vision of sunshine and carefree smiles. "Like chasing butterflies in the park? That makes me happy!"

Their father chuckled, the sound warm and genuine. "Exactly, Aarika! But for others," he continued, his voice turning thoughtful, "the meaning of life lies in helping others, in making the world a better place than they found it."

He gestured towards the window, where a volunteer was handing out food to the homeless man they'd seen earlier. "See that kind lady, Aarika? Maybe for her, the meaning of life is in that simple act of kindness, in easing someone's burden."

Paarth, a hint of determination creeping into his voice, asked, "So, is it about achieving big things, like becoming a superhero or an astronaut?"

Their father's smile broadened. "Those are great dreams, Paarth! But the meaning of life can also be found in the small moments, in learning new things, in the connections we make with others."

He looked at them, his gaze filled with a love so profound it shone in his eyes. "For me," he said, his voice thick with emotion, "The meaning of life is about living a good life, being kind to others, and making a positive impact on the world, no matter how small."

Aarika, her brow furrowed in concentration, chimed in, "So, it's different for everyone, Papa? Like a puzzle with different pieces for each person?"

Their father nodded, his eyes twinkling with pride at their growing understanding. "Exactly, Aarika! It's a personal journey, a story you write with your choices and actions. And the beauty lies in the exploration, in discovering what makes your heart sing, what makes you feel like you're contributing to something bigger than yourself."

From that day on, Aarika and Paarth saw the world not as a destination, but as a vast canvas waiting to be painted with the colours of their purpose. They looked at their experiences, from helping a lost puppy find its way home to diligently practicing their piano lessons, with a newfound appreciation. The world became a stage where they could experiment, explore, and discover what truly mattered to them. And while the allure of a phone and the thrill of video games remained, they were now accompanied by a burning desire to find their own meaning, a testament to the beauty of a life yet to be written, a life filled with purpose, exploration, and the endless possibilities that awaited them on their personal journeys.

■■■

CHAPTER 35

WHY DO BAD THINGS HAPPEN?

A tear escaped Aarika's eye, tracing a glistening path down her cheek. Her lower lip trembled as she clutched her stuffed bunny, its worn fur offering little comfort against the storm brewing inside her.

"Papa," she whimpered, her voice choked with emotion, "Why did Goldie have to go to sleep forever?"

Their beloved goldfish, Goldie, had been a silent companion for as long as Aarika could remember. Now, floating listlessly at the bottom of the bowl, he was a stark reminder of life's impermanence.

Paarth, usually boisterous, sat beside her, his brow furrowed in confusion. The world seemed to lose its colour, the playful banter of the afternoon replaced by a heavy silence.

Their father knelt before them, his presence a comforting lighthouse in the sea of their grief. He pulled them both into a warm embrace, a silent acknowledgment of their pain.

"Bad things happen sometimes, Aarika," he began, his voice laced with a quiet empathy that soothed their trembling hearts. "Things that feel unfair and leave us feeling lost, like a ship without a sail."

Aarika sniffled, burying her face in his shirt. "But why, Papa? Why Goldie?"

Her father sighed, a tremor of sadness echoing in his voice. "There are many reasons, Aarika. Sometimes, it's like a storm brewing in the sky, something beyond our control."

He reached out and gently stroked Paarth's hair. "It can be because of the choices people make, or even natural occurrences, like a strong wind that knocks down a tree."

Paarth, a flicker of anger sparking in his eyes, clenched his fists. "But it's not fair! Goldie didn't do anything wrong."

Their father nodded, his gaze filled with understanding. "You're right, Paarth. It doesn't feel fair. It's okay to be angry and to feel sad. But even in darkness, there can be a spark of light."

He gestured towards the window, where a group of volunteers were planting trees in the park. "See those people, Aarika? They're planting new trees to replace the ones lost in the storm. Even though bad things happen, we can always find ways to make things better."

Aarika, a sliver of hope peeking through her tears, asked, "So, we can help others who are sad too?"

Their father smiled, a beacon of warmth in the gloom. "Exactly, Aarika! We can't always control what happens, but we can choose how we respond. We can learn from our experiences, grow stronger, and even help others facing their own storms."

From that day on, Aarika and Paarth saw the world not just as a place of sunshine and rainbows, but as a tapestry woven with threads of joy and sorrow. They approached difficult experiences not with fear, but with a newfound resilience. They learned to find solace in helping others, in offering a hug to a friend who lost a pet, or a helping hand to a neighbor cleaning up after a storm. The world, though sometimes unfair, held the potential for growth, compassion, and the act of making a difference, a testament to the enduring human spirit that could rise above even the darkest of times. And while the allure of other exciting things in their life remained, they were now accompanied by a newfound strength, a determination to face life's challenges head-on, and a heart brimming with compassion for those around them.

■■■

CHAPTER 36

WHY DO I HAVE TO GO TO BED EARLY?

A yawn escaped Aarika's lips, a wide, watery one that stretched from her ear to ear. She rubbed her fists into her eyes, battling the urge to surrender to the comfortable pull of sleep. But bedtime, that unwelcome visitor, had arrived, casting a long shadow over her evening.

"Papa," she whined, her voice thick with sleep and a hint of defiance, "Why do we have to go to bed so early? Can't we just play for a little longer?"

Across the room, Paarth echoed her sentiment, his voice laced with frustration. He bounced on the balls of his feet, a ball of barely contained energy threatening to burst. "Yeah, Papa! Just one more game, then we'll promise to go to bed!"

Their father, a familiar warmth radiating from his eyes, met their gazes with a gentle smile. He understood the allure of staying up late, the siren song of one more story, one more game. But he also knew the importance of a good night's sleep, a silent guardian of their health and well-being.

He sat down on the edge of their bed, pulling them both into a hug. The embrace, a silent promise of comfort and understanding, calmed the storm of protest brewing within them.

"I know bedtime can feel like the worst monster under the bed sometimes, Aarika," he began, his voice laced with a quiet empathy. "It cuts short all the fun, all the laughter."

Aarika sniffled, her eyelids drooping despite her best efforts. "But bedtime is actually a kind monster, in disguise," their father continued, a twinkle in his eye. "It helps your body rest, like a superhero recharging their powers for the next adventure."

He reached out and gently tucked a stray strand of hair behind Paarth's ear. "Just like your favourite video game characters, Paarth, your body needs time to recharge. Sleep helps you grow strong and healthy, so you can run faster, jump higher, and learn all sorts of amazing things."

Aarika, a sliver of curiosity peeking through her sleepiness, asked, "So, sleep makes us like superheroes?"

Their father's smile widened. "Exactly, Aarika! When you get enough sleep, you wake up feeling refreshed and ready to conquer the day. You can concentrate better in school, remember all the cool things you learn, and have even more energy to play with your friends."

He gestured towards the window, where the first stars were beginning to twinkle in the darkening sky. "Think of sleep like a magical night potion, Aarika. It whisks you away to a dreamland adventure, and when you wake up in the morning, you're ready to face a whole new day of fun and exploration."

Paarth, a hint of understanding replacing his frustration, leaned against his father. "So, if we go to bed early, we'll have more energy to play tomorrow?"

Their father chuckled, the sound warm and reassuring. "Exactly, Paarth! Plus, who knows what kind of amazing dreams you might have tonight? Maybe you'll even fly like a superhero or explore a new world in your sleep."

From that day on, Aarika and Paarth saw bedtime not as a punishment, but as a necessary pit stop on their grand adventure. They embraced their bedtime routines, the warm baths, the gentle stories, with a newfound appreciation. Sleep became a gateway to a world of possibilities, a time for their bodies and minds to recharge, preparing them for the endless adventures that awaited them with the rising sun. And while the other allures of life remained, they were now accompanied by a newfound understanding of the importance of sleep, a testament to the power of transforming bedtime from a foe to a friend, a key to unlocking their full potential.

■■■

CHAPTER 37

WHY DO WE NEED MONEY?

Aarika's eyes widened as she stared at the shiny new toy car in the store window. Its sleek red paint gleamed under the lights, beckoning her with the promise of endless imaginative adventures. But a frown creased her forehead, a shadow of confusion darkening her usually bright face.

"Papa," she tugged on his shirt, her voice barely a whisper, "Why can't we buy that car? I really, really want it. I have my pocket money."

Paarth, ever the echo of his sister's desires, chimed in, his lower lip trembling slightly. "Yeah, Papa! It has cool flames and everything. Can't we just get it?"

Their father knelt before them, his gaze filled with a gentle understanding. He knew the yearning in their hearts, the powerful pull of a coveted toy. But he also knew the responsibility that came with money, the silent language of value and exchange.

"Money can be a tricky thing, Aarika," he began, his voice laced with a quiet empathy. "It's like a special kind of magic dust, a way to get things we need and want."

Aarika's frown deepened. "Magic dust? But it doesn't look like dust at all!"

Her father chuckled, the sound warm and reassuring. "Not exactly, Aarika. Money is more like a way of trading. We use it to buy things, like food to fill our tummies and clothes to keep us comfortable."

He reached into his pocket and pulled out a single coin, its worn surface glinting in the sunlight. "See this, Paarth? This coin represents a tiny bit of work someone did, a service they provided."

Paarth, his brow furrowed in concentration, took the coin gently in his hand. "So, we give this coin to the store lady, and then she gives us the car?"

Their father nodded, a hint of sadness flickering in his eyes. "Not quite, Paarth. We only have a limited amount of this magic dust, and we have to use it wisely. We need some for food, some for rent, and some for other important things."

He looked at the car in the window, its red paint seeming a little less vibrant now. "This car might be really cool, Aarika, but there might be other things we need more right now. Maybe new shoes for school, or healthy groceries."

Aarika, a flicker of understanding replacing her disappointment, looked back at the car with a newfound perspective. "So, we can't always get everything we want, even if it's shiny and red?"

Her father pulled her into a hug, the warmth of his embrace a silent comfort. "Exactly, Aarika. But that's okay. It helps us learn to appreciate what we do have, to be creative, and maybe even find something even more special with the magic dust we have left."

From that day on, Aarika and Paarth saw money not just as a means to an end, but as a tool for making thoughtful choices. They began to understand the concept of budgeting, of prioritizing needs over wants. They learned to appreciate the value of hard work, the effort behind every coin their parents earned. The shiny red car in the window remained a distant dream, but it was replaced by a newfound respect for money, a growing sense of responsibility, and the spark of creativity that led them to invent their own imaginative games with simple objects around the house. And while the allure and the thrill of new toys remained, they were now accompanied by a valuable lesson in delayed gratification, a testament to the power of understanding the world of economics, not through magic dust, but through responsibility and thoughtful choices.

■■■

CHAPTER 38

HOW DO CARS WORK?

Aarika's eyes sparkled with curiosity as she stood beside the gleaming black car parked in their driveway. It wasn't the fancy sports car from the store window, but it was theirs, a source of endless fascination and wonder.

“Papa,” she tugged on his shirt, her voice brimming with excitement, “How does this car work? How does it move by itself?”

Paarth, mirroring his sister's enthusiasm, bounced on the balls of his feet. “Yeah, Papa! Is there a giant invisible horse pulling it? Like in the storybooks?”

Their father chuckled, the sound warm and inviting. He knelt before them, his presence a comforting anchor in their sea of questions.

“Cars aren't pulled by horses, Paarth,” he began, his voice laced with a quiet amusement. “They're powered by something much more fascinating – a bit of controlled magic, if you will.”

Aarika's eyes widened. “Magic? Like the spells in our fairytales?”

Her father's smile widened. “Not exactly, Aarika. But it is a kind of magic, the magic of science and engineering.”

He reached out and gently placed a hand on the hood of the car. “Underneath all this shiny metal,” he explained, his voice filled with a quiet reverence, “lies a mighty heart – the engine.”

Paarth scrunched up his nose in confusion. “An engine? But where? I don't see any hearts!”

Their father gestured towards the front of the car. "It's hidden here, Paarth. This engine burns a special kind of fuel, like a potion that gives the car energy."

He crouched down to their eye level, his gaze filled with a playful glint. "Imagine this fuel turning into tiny explosions, a controlled rumble that pushes the car forward. It's like a tiny dragon living inside, breathing fire to make the car move!"

Aarika giggled, the image of a fire-breathing dragon replacing the engine a delightful twist on reality. "So, the fire pushes on the wheels, and that's how the car moves?"

Their father nodded, his smile turning genuine. "Exactly, Aarika! But there's more to this magic. There's a special gearbox, like a conductor in an orchestra, that controls the flow of this fiery energy to the wheels."

He reached out and pointed to the brakes. "And these, Aarika, are like the guardians of the car. They slow it down and stop it when needed, like a superhero cape that slows down your fall during playtime."

Paarth, his imagination ignited, chimed in, "So, the car is like a big, strong creature with a fiery heart, a conductor telling it what to do, and special shoes to stop it from running away?"

Their father's laughter echoed in the driveway, a warm sound that filled the air. "In a way, Paarth, you're not that far off! Cars are complex machines, but when you break it down, it's like a symphony of parts working together to take us on adventures."

From that day on, Aarika and Paarth saw cars not just as vehicles, but as marvels of engineering, testaments to human ingenuity. Every ride became a journey of discovery, a chance to imagine the dragon roaring beneath the hood, the conductor keeping the rhythm, and the trusty brakes ensuring a safe arrival. Their fascination with cars grew into a passion for learning about mechanics, a curiosity that fueled their desire to one day peek under the hood and witness the magic first hand. And while the allure of car video games and the thrill of imaginary races remained, they were now accompanied by a newfound appreciation for the wonder of science, a spark of curiosity that ignited a love for learning that would propel them forward on countless adventures to come.

■■■

CHAPTER 39

WHY ARE ANTS RED?

Aarika's tiny finger pointed at the trail of crimson specks marching across the kitchen counter. Her eyes widened with a mix of fascination and disgust. "Papa, why are these ants red?" she asked, her voice laced with curiosity.

Paarth, ever the curious companion, joined the investigation, his face scrunched up in concentration. "Maybe they ate some red paint?" he suggested, his eyes sparkling with a mischievous glint.

Their father chuckled, the warm sound a comforting anchor amidst the tiny red invaders. "Not quite, Paarth," he said, kneeling to join their miniature scientific expedition. "Ants come in different colours, just like people."

Aarika's eyes widened in surprise. "Ants have different colours? I've only ever seen black ones!"

Their father nodded. "You're right, Aarika. Black ants are the most common ones we see, but there are also red ants, brown ants, and even some that are yellow."

Paarth, undeterred by the lack of paint-eating ants, continued his investigation. "So, why are these ones red? Are they special?"

Their father smiled. "They might feel special to you, Paarth. But the colour of an ant is just like the colour of your hair or eyes. It's part of their natural look."

Aarika, her curiosity insatiable, pressed further. "But why red? It's not a very good hiding colour."

Their father chuckled again. "That's a very good point, Aarika. The colour of an ant doesn't always have a specific reason. Sometimes, it's just how they are."

He scooped up a small red ant onto a piece of paper, holding it gently for them to observe. "See, even though it's red, it's still an ant. It has six legs, tiny antennas, and it's working hard to carry food back to its nest."

Aarika's eyes softened as she watched the tiny creature scurry across the paper. "It's kind of cute," she admitted, her fear of the red invaders slowly dissipating.

Paarth, ever the protector, gently placed the paper back on the counter, allowing the ant to continue its journey. "We should let it go back to its friends," he declared, a newfound respect for the tiny creature.

As they watched the ant disappear back into the crack in the countertop, Aarika and Paarth felt a sense of wonder and respect for the tiny creatures that shared their world. The red ants were no longer just creepy crawlies; they were fascinating beings, each with its own story to tell.

■■■

CHAPTER 40

WHY DO RED ANTS BITE AND BLACK DON'T?

The afternoon sun streamed through the kitchen window, casting dancing shadows on the countertop. Paarth, his brow furrowed in concentration, hovered his small hand over a trail of red ants, their tiny legs a blur as they marched with unwavering purpose. Aarika, her eyes wide with curiosity, mimicked their movements with her own tiny fingers, her brow mirroring her brother's.

"Papa," Paarth whispered, his voice filled with a mixture of fascination and apprehension, "why do these ants bite? The black ones don't." He glanced at his father, seeking an explanation.

Their father, observing the children with a warm smile, knelt beside them. "That's a very good question, Paarth," he said, his voice gentle. "You know, ants, like us, have different personalities. Some are shy and prefer to keep to themselves, while others are a bit more...spirited."

Paarth's eyes widened. "So, the red ones are the bullies?"

Their father chuckled. "Not exactly bullies, Paarth. Think of it like this. Some people are shy, while others are more outgoing. It's the same with ants. Red ants tend to be a bit more protective of their homes. Imagine if someone suddenly barged into your room – you might feel a little scared too, right?"

Aarika, her face wrinkling in thought, nodded vigorously. "Yeah," she agreed, "I'd probably hide under my blanket!"

Paarth giggled, picturing the scene. "Me too! I'd shout 'Go away!' and throw my toys at them."

Their father smiled. "See? It's the same with the ants. They're just trying to protect their home and their families. They might give a little nip if they feel threatened, but it's not because they're mean."

Aarika, her eyes softening, looked at the ants with newfound sympathy. "Poor ants. Maybe they're just scared."

Their father nodded. "It's possible, Aarika. They're much smaller than us, and we can be quite big and scary to them. Imagine if a giant suddenly appeared in your room – you might feel a little scared too, right?"

Paarth and Aarika shuddered dramatically. "Yeah," Paarth admitted, "I'd probably want to hide under my blanket."

Their father chuckled. "Exactly. So, let's try to understand them. They're just trying to survive, like us." He pointed to a particularly large ant struggling to carry a crumb that looked almost as big as itself. "Look at that one! He's a strong worker, carrying a heavy load."

Paarth watched the ant with wide eyes. "He must be tired," he said, his voice filled with concern.

"He probably is," their father agreed. "But he's determined to get that food back to his colony. Ants work together as a team, just like a family."

Aarika, her curiosity piqued, asked, "What kind of food do they eat?"

"Oh, all sorts of things!" their father replied. "Crumbs, tiny insects, even sweet liquids like honeydew." He pointed to a tiny droplet of something glistening on the counter. "See that? That might be honeydew. It's a sweet substance that some insects produce."

Paarth leaned closer, his eyes following the ants as they marched towards the droplet. "They're going to have a feast!" he exclaimed.

As they watched the ants continue their relentless march, a sense of wonder and respect for these tiny creatures began to grow within Paarth and Aarika. They realized that these red ants, despite their small size, were a complex and fascinating society, just like their own family. And while a bite might be unpleasant, it was essential to understand that the ants were not inherently malicious, but simply trying to navigate their world, just as they were.

With newfound respect, they watched the ants disappear beneath the fridge, their tiny world hidden from view. It was a small moment, a fleeting encounter with nature, but it was one that would stay with them, a reminder of the interconnectedness of all living things and the importance of understanding and empathy, not just towards humans, but towards all creatures, big and small.

■■■

CHAPTER 41
WHY DO FLIES EXIST?

The afternoon sun was bright and scorching hot, illuminating dust motes dancing in the air. Aarika swatted at the buzzing fly circling her head, her eyes narrowed in frustration. "Why do flies even exist, Papa?" she grumbled, her voice laced with annoyance. "They're just buzzing around, being gross!"

Paarth, ever curious, joined the battle, his tiny hands making futile attempts to swat the pesky insect. "Yeah, they're so annoying!" he exclaimed, his voice rising in pitch. He puffed out his chest, mimicking a superhero, "I'll defeat this fly!"

Their father smiled, tempering the children's growing irritation. He lowered himself to their level, his gaze filled with gentle understanding. "Flies, like all living things, have a role to play in our world," he began, his voice soothing the growing storm of their annoyance.

Aarika scoffed. "But they're just gross! They land on garbage and… other things!"

Their father nodded, acknowledging her feelings. "They can be, Aarika. They can carry germs and be a nuisance. But even the things we find unpleasant have a purpose."

Paarth, his curiosity piqued, asked, "Like what, Papa?"

"Well," their father began, "flies help break down decaying matter. Think of them as nature's little clean-up crew. They help decompose things like fallen leaves and dead animals, returning nutrients to the soil."

Aarika's eyes widened in disbelief. "So, they're actually helpful?"

Their father smiled. "In their own way, yes. They're part of a big ecosystem, a complex puzzle where every piece has a role to play. Just like bees help pollinate flowers and butterflies spread seeds, flies play a vital role in the circle of life."

A moment of silence fell over the room as the children contemplated this new perspective. The buzzing fly, once a symbol of annoyance, now seemed to hold a tiny bit of fascination.

“But they still shouldn't land on our food,” Aarika declared, a stubborn streak emerging.

Their father laughed. “Agreed, Aarika. That's where our role comes in. We can protect our food, keep our surroundings clean, and coexist peacefully with these little creatures. We can learn to understand their role in the world while also taking steps to protect ourselves.”

As the fly buzzed closer, Paarth and Aarika exchanged a determined glance. Together, they devised a plan to outsmart the pesky insect. Paarth, armed with a rolled-up newspaper, pretended to be a fearsome knight, while Aarika, wielding a brightly colored fly swatter, acted as his valiant squire. They giggled as they chased the fly around the kitchen, their laughter echoing through the room.

Finally, with a triumphant whoop, Paarth managed to swat the fly. But instead of celebrating, he and Aarika looked at the fallen insect with a newfound respect. They had learned a valuable lesson that day – even the smallest creatures have a purpose, and understanding that purpose can help us appreciate the intricate balance of nature.

Later, as they washed their hands, Paarth asked, “Papa, what other creatures have important roles we don't always see?”

Their father smiled. “That's a wonderful question, Paarth! We can learn about all sorts of amazing creatures and the important jobs they do. We can even visit a nearby park and observe insects in their natural habitat.”

Paarth and Aarika, their initial annoyance replaced with curiosity, eagerly agreed. They knew their adventure with the fly was just the beginning of their journey to understand the wonders of the natural world.

■■■

CHAPTER 42

WHERE IS THAT JADIBOOTI THAT HANUMAN JI HELD IN HIS HANDS AS A MOUNTAIN?

The bright LED lamp cast dancing shadows on the worn wooden floor. Aarika, her eyes sparkling with an otherworldly gleam, pointed at the old illustrated Ramayana on the dining table. Her finger traced the image of Hanuman, the mighty monkey God, holding aloft a colossal mountain.

"Papa," she asked, her voice filled with wonder, "Where did Hanuman get that magical herb to heal Lord Ram's younger brother Shree Lakshman?"

Paarth, the curious companion, leaned in closer, his eyes mirroring his sister's fascination. "And how did he carry such a big mountain?" he added, his voice filled with awe.

Their father chuckled, a warm sound that filled the room. He sat beside them, his gaze filled with a gentle understanding. "That's a fantastic question, my little explorers," he began, his voice laced with a hint of adventure. "Hanumanji's journey to find the Sanjeevani Booti is one of the most epic quests in our cultural heritage."

Aarika's eyes widened. "A real-life superhero story?" she exclaimed, her voice filled with excitement.

Their father nodded, his eyes twinkling with amusement. "Indeed, Aarika. Hanumanji was not just a monkey; he was a symbol of strength, devotion, and unwavering determination. He faced countless obstacles, flew across vast distances, and even battled demons to retrieve the life-saving herb."

Paarth, his imagination ignited, asked, "Do you think there are still magical herbs like that in the world?"

Their father paused, his expression turning thoughtful. "While we haven't discovered any magical herbs that can heal like the Sanjeevani Booti, there are countless plants and herbs with incredible healing properties. Scientists are constantly exploring the natural world, discovering new medicines and treatments."

He pointed to a vibrant butterfly flitting across the garden. "Look at that butterfly, Aarika. Its wings are a masterpiece of nature. Some butterflies use their colors to warn predators, while others use them to attract mates. Each creature, each plant, has a unique purpose, a role to play in the delicate balance of nature."

Aarika's face lit up with hope. "Maybe we can find a magical herb too!" she exclaimed, her eyes sparkling with determination.

Their father smiled. "That's the spirit of adventure, Aarika! While we might not find a mountain-sized herb, we can certainly explore the world around us, learn about different plants, and appreciate the wonders of nature. Let's go on a little adventure of our own!"

He led them into the garden, a weathered magnifying glass in his hand. "Let's see what secrets this little corner of the world holds," he said, his voice filled with excitement.

Paarth and Aarika, armed with their magnifying glasses, embarked on their own mini-quest. They examined the vibrant blooms of the hibiscus, the delicate petals of the rose, and the spiky leaves of the aloe vera. Their father explained the different parts of each plant, their uses, and their role in the ecosystem.

As the sun began to set, casting long shadows across the garden, they returned to the house, their minds filled with newfound knowledge and a sense of wonder. They had not found a magical herb, but they had discovered a different kind of magic – the magic of exploration, the joy of discovery, and the deep connection between themselves, their family, and the natural world.

That evening, as they snuggled into their beds, the image of Hanumanji's heroic journey lingered in their minds. They knew that their own adventure had just begun. The world, with its countless mysteries and wonders, was waiting to be explored, one plant, one discovery, at a time.

■■■

CHAPTER 43:

WHY DO WORMS LIKE TO STAY INSIDE EARTH?

Aarika's tiny finger poked at the wriggling creature, her eyes wide with curiosity mixed with a hint of disgust. "Papa, why do worms like to stay inside the earth?" she asked, her voice laced with wonder.

Paarth, the brave explorer, leaned closer, his fascination overcoming his initial sickness. "Yeah, it's dark and yucky down there," he added, his voice filled with a mix of curiosity and concern.

Their father smiled, a warm sound that filled the room. He knelt beside them, his gaze filled with gentle understanding. "Worms have a very important job, you know," he began, his voice soothing the growing curiosity of his children.

Aarika's eyes sparkled. "Are they like little helpers?" she asked, her voice filled with excitement.

Their father nodded. "Exactly. They are nature's tiny farmers. They help to aerate the soil, which means they help the air get to the roots of plants."

Paarth's brow furrowed in concentration. "So, they're like superheroes for plants?" he asked, his voice filled with admiration.

"You could say that," their father replied, a smile gracing his lips. "They also help break down dead leaves and other organic matter, turning them into rich soil that helps plants grow."

Aarika's face softened. "They're like little gardeners!" she exclaimed, her voice filled with newfound respect.

Their father nodded, his eyes filled with pride. "Just like you two are little explorers, discovering new things every day. Worms are exploring their own world underground, doing their important job."

As they watched the worm continue its journey, a sense of wonder filled the room. The tiny creature, once a source of disgust, had become a fascinating subject of study. They realized that even the smallest living thing had a vital role to play in the grand scheme of nature.

■■■

CHAPTER 44

IF THE SUN IS SO FAR AWAY, WHY DO WE FEEL HEAT, AND HOW DO WE GET SUNLIGHT?

Aarika squinted against the bright sunlight streaming through the window, her small hand shading her eyes. "Papa, the sun is so far away, but it's so hot," she exclaimed, her voice filled with a mix of wonder and confusion.

Paarth, the curious companion, joined her, tilting his head to examine the sun's rays. "Yeah, it's like a giant fire in the sky," he added, his eyes wide with awe.

Their father kind of giggled. He knelt beside them, his gaze filled with gentle understanding. "That's a great question, my little scientists," he began, his voice laced with a hint of excitement. "The sun is indeed very far away, but it's also incredibly powerful."

Aarika's eyes sparkled. "Like a superhero?" she asked, her imagination taking flight.

Their father smiled. "You could say that. The sun is like a massive ball of super-hot gas, releasing energy in the form of light and heat."

Paarth's eyebrow furrowed in concentration. "So, it's like a giant lightbulb?" he asked, his voice filled with curiosity.

"That's a good comparison, Paarth," their father replied. "But imagine a lightbulb that's millions of times brighter and hotter. The light and heat travel through space and reach us here on Earth in the form of sunlight."

Aarika's eyes widened in amazement. "So, the sunlight is like a magic blanket that keeps us warm?"

Their father nodded, his eyes twinkling with amusement. "You could say that, Aarika. The sunlight warms the Earth, and that warmth is what keeps us cozy."

As they continued to bask in the sun's warmth, a sense of wonder filled the room. The once distant and abstract concept of the sun had become a tangible force, a source of life and energy. They realized that the sun, though far away, had a profound impact on their lives, from the warmth they felt on their skin to the food they ate. It was a connection that went beyond sight, a reminder of the vastness and interconnectedness of the universe.

■■■

CHAPTER 45

IS THERE ANY PLANET X?

Aarika's eyes sparkled with a mix of curiosity and wonder as she gazed up at the night sky, her small finger pointing at a distant twinkle. "Papa, is there a planet X?" she asked, her voice filled with a sense of adventure.

Paarth, ever the explorer, joined her, his eyes scanning the celestial expanse. "Like a secret planet?" he asked, his voice filled with excitement.

Their father chuckled, the warm sound a comforting anchor in the room filled with starry dreams. "That's a fantastic question, my little astronomers," he began, his voice laced with a hint of mystery. "Planet X, or Planet Nine as scientists call it, is a hypothetical planet that some astronomers believe might exist at the edge of our solar system."

Aarika's eyes widened in disbelief. "A whole new planet? That's like finding a secret treasure!" she exclaimed, her voice filled with excitement.

Paarth's imagination took flight. "Can we go there on a spaceship?" he asked, his voice brimming with childlike wonder.

Their father smiled. "While we can't visit Planet X just yet, scientists are using powerful telescopes to look for it. It's a thrilling adventure, exploring the unknown, just like your favorite superheroes."

Aarika's face lit up with determination. "Maybe we can discover a new planet someday!" she declared, her voice filled with a sense of purpose.

Their father's heart swelled with pride. "Who knows, Aarika? With your curiosity and Paarth's adventurous spirit, anything is possible."

As they continued to gaze at the night sky, a sense of wonder and possibility filled the room. The idea of a hidden planet, waiting to be discovered, ignited their imaginations, fueling their dreams of becoming future explorers and scientists. It was a moment that would stay with them, a reminder that even in the vastness of the universe, there was always room for new discoveries and endless adventures.

■■■

CHAPTER 46

IN OUR SOLAR SYSTEM WHAT SPEED DO ALL PLANETS ROTATE?

Aarika's eyes were wide with wonder as she gazed up at the night sky, her small finger tracing an imaginary path across the celestial canvas. "Papa," she asked, her voice filled with a mix of excitement and confusion, "How fast do the planets spin?"

Paarth, the curious companion, joined her, his eyes scanning the heavens for answers. "Yeah, and why don't we fall off if they're spinning so fast?" he added, his voice laced with a hint of concern.

Their father amused, with warmth knelt beside them, his gaze filled with a gentle understanding. "That's a fantastic question, my little astronauts," he began, his voice laced with a hint of adventure. "Each planet spins at its own unique speed, like dancers in a cosmic ballet."

Aarika's eyes sparkled with excitement. "So, some planets are faster dancers than others?" she asked, her imagination taking flight.

Their father smiled. "Exactly, Aarika. Jupiter, for instance, is a very fast spinner, while Venus takes its time."

Paarth's eyebrows wrinkled in concentration. "But why don't we fall off the Earth when it's spinning so fast?" he asked, his voice filled with a genuine sense of amaze.

Their father took a deep breath, preparing to unravel the cosmic mystery. "That's a brilliant question, Paarth. The Earth is incredibly large, and we're tiny compared to it. So, even though it's spinning very fast, we're moving at the same speed as the Earth, so we don't feel it."

Aarika's eyes widened in amazement. "We're flying through space?" she exclaimed, her voice filled with a mix of excitement and disbelief.

Their father nodded, his eyes twinkling with amusement. "In a way, yes. We're all passengers on a spaceship called Earth, traveling through the vastness of space."

As they continued to gaze up at the night sky, a sense of awe and wonder washed over them. The once familiar celestial bodies had transformed into a mesmerizing cosmic dance, a symphony of motion and gravity. It was a moment they would cherish, a spark ignited in their minds that would fuel their future explorations of the universe.

■■■

CHAPTER 47

WHY ARE NEPTUNE OR URANUS SO COLD?

Aarika shivered, her breath visible in the cold winter air as she gazed up at the night sky. "Papa, why are Neptune and Uranus so cold?" she asked, her voice small against the vast expanse of the universe.

Paarth, ever the curious companion, rubbed his arms for warmth. "Yeah, it's like living in a giant freezer out there," he added, his voice filled with a mix of wonder and disbelief.

Their father chuckled, a warm sound that cut through the chill. "That's a great question, my little astronauts," he began, his voice filled with a gentle enthusiasm. "Neptune and Uranus are incredibly far from the sun, much farther than Earth."

Aarika's eyes widened in surprise. "So they're like lonely planets?" she asked, her voice filled with sympathy.

Their father smiled. "In a way, yes. The farther a planet is from the sun, the colder it gets. It's like standing closer or farther away from a campfire."

Paarth's brow furrowed in concentration. "But why can't they just move closer to the sun, like we move closer to the heater?" he asked, his voice filled with a childlike logic.

Their father laughed. "The planets are held in place by a powerful force called gravity, which keeps them in their orbits. It's like being stuck on a giant cosmic rollercoaster."

Aarika's imagination took flight. "So, they're like ice cream planets?" she asked, her eyes sparkling with delight.

Their father chuckled. "In a way, yes. But remember, those planets are made mostly of gases, not ice cream. It's a cold, icy world out there."

As they continued to gaze at the night sky, a sense of awe and wonder filled the room. The once distant and abstract concept of planetary temperatures had become a tangible experience, a reminder of the vastness and diversity of the universe. It was a moment they would cherish, a spark ignited in their minds that would fuel their future explorations of the cosmos.

■■■

CHAPTER 48

WHY CAN'T ANYONE CLIMB MOUNT KAILASH?

Aarika's eyes sparkled with wonder as she pointed towards a picture of Mount Kailash in a geography book. "Papa, why can't anyone climb that mountain?" she asked, her voice filled with a mix of curiosity and awe.

Paarth, ever the explorer, leaned in closer, his eyes scanning the image with a sense of adventure. "Yeah, it looks like a giant ice cream cone," he said, his voice filled with childlike wonder.

Their father chuckled, a warm sound that filled the room. He knelt beside them, his gaze filled with a gentle understanding. "Mount Kailash is a truly special place, my little explorers," he began, his voice laced with a hint of reverence.

Aarika's eyes widened with excitement. "Is it a magical mountain?" she asked, her imagination taking flight.

Their father smiled. "While it's not magical in the traditional sense, it certainly holds a special place in many hearts," he replied. "It's considered sacred by several religions, including Hinduism, Buddhism, and Jainism."

Paarth's brow furrowed in concentration. "So, people don't climb it because it's special?" he asked, his voice filled with respect.

Their father nodded. "That's part of it. But it's also an incredibly challenging mountain to climb. The weather is harsh, the terrain is treacherous, and the altitude is extreme. It's a place that demands respect."

Aarika's eyes filled with a sense of awe. "Is it like a giant guardian of the world," she whispered, her voice filled with reverence.

Their father smiled. "In a way, yes. Mount Kailash is a symbol of the mysteries that still surround our world. It's a reminder that there are still places untouched by human hands, places that inspire wonder and respect."

As they continued to look at the picture, a sense of reverence filled the room. The once distant mountain had become a symbol of mystery and wonder, a place that ignited their imaginations and sparked a desire to explore and learn more about the world around them.

■■■

CHAPTER 49

WHAT CAME BEFORE – EGG OR CHICKEN?

The summer sun poured into the living room, casting long, dancing shadows that seemed to mock the somber question hanging in the air. Paarth and Aarika sat side by side on the worn, floral-patterned couch, their small hands clasped together. Their eyes, usually filled with a childlike wonder, were now clouded with a mix of confusion and fear.

"Papa," Paarth began, his voice barely a whisper. "What came first – the egg or the chicken?"

Aarika nodded, her eyes fixed on the floor. "I think the egg."

Their father sighed, his heart aching. He had hoped to shield his children from the harsh realities of the world, but it seemed their innocence was slowly fading. He took a deep breath and tried to find the right words.

"Well, Paarth and Aarika," he began, his voice gentle, "that's a very old question with no easy answer."

Paarth's eyes widened. "Why not?"

The man smiled sadly. "It's a riddle that scientists have been trying to solve for centuries. Some people believe that the egg came first, because chickens evolved from other birds that laid eggs."

Aarika looked up, her eyes filled with hope. "But where did the first egg come from?"

The man nodded. "That's the mystery. Some scientists believe that the first egg was laid by a bird that was not quite a chicken yet."

Paarth thought for a moment. "So, it's like a puzzle?"

The man squeezed his children's hands. "Exactly. It's a puzzle that may never be solved. But that's the beauty of it. It's a question that has sparked curiosity and debate for centuries."

As the sun began to set, casting long shadows across the room, Paarth and Aarika felt a sense of excitement wash over them. They knew they couldn't change the world overnight, but they were determined to explore the mysteries of the universe.

■■■

CHAPTER 50

WHY DO WE GET STUCK IN SAND?

Aarika's tiny feet sank into the warm, yielding sand, her laughter echoing as she chased the playful waves. But suddenly, her laughter turned to a yelp as her foot became firmly stuck. “Papa, I'm stuck!” she cried out, her eyes wide with panic.

Paarth, the brave explorer, rushed to her aid, but his foot too met with the same sandy resistance. “We're stuck!” he exclaimed, his voice filled with a mix of frustration and amusement.

Their father chuckled, a warm sound that soothed their growing panic. “Ah, the sandy trap,” he said, kneeling down to help them. “Sand is tricky like that.”

Aarika's face scrunched up in frustration. “But why?” she demanded, her voice filled with indignation. “It's just sand!”

Their father smiled gently. “Sand is made up of tiny, loose particles. When you step on it, the grains shift and create a kind of vacuum around your foot. It's like quicksand, but not quite as dramatic.”

Paarth's eyes widened in amazement. “So, we're actually stuck in a tiny vacuum?” he asked, his voice filled with a mix of fear and fascination.

“Not exactly a vacuum, but close,” their father replied. “It's a bit like trying to walk on a bed of marbles. The more you struggle, the deeper you sink.”

With gentle encouragement, their father helped them wiggle their feet free, the sandy prison finally releasing its captives. As they stood up, covered in sand but filled with a renewed sense of adventure, they looked at each other and burst into laughter. The sandy surprise had turned into a memorable experience, a testament to the unpredictable nature of the natural world.

■■■

CHAPTER 51

WHY ARE TOMATOES RED?

Aarika's tiny hand reached out to pluck a ripe tomato from their grandma's garden, her eyes sparkling with anticipation. "Papa, why is this tomato red?" she asked, her voice filled with curiosity.

Paarth, ever the curious companion, took a moment to examine the tomato, his finger tracing its smooth skin. "Maybe it's because it's shy," he suggested, a mischievous glint in his eye.

Their father chuckled, a warm sound that filled the garden. "That's a creative thought, Paarth," he replied, kneeling down to their level. "Tomatoes turn red because of a special pigment called lycopene."

Aarika's eyes widened in confusion. "What's a pigment?" she asked, her voice filled with wonder.

Their father explained, "A pigment is like a tiny artist that colours things. Lycopene is the artist that makes tomatoes red. It's a sign that the tomato is ripe and ready to eat."

Paarth's eyebrow furrowed in concentration. "So, if it wasn't red, it wouldn't be good to eat?" he asked, his voice filled with concern.

Their father nodded. "Usually, yes. The red colour is nature's way of telling us the tomato is ripe and sweet. But it's always a good idea to ask a grown-up before tasting something new."

Aarika's eyes sparkled with excitement. "Let's plant some tomato seeds and watch them grow red!" she exclaimed, her imagination taking flight.

Their father smiled. "That's a wonderful idea, Aarika. We can learn so much by observing nature firsthand."

As they continued to explore the garden, their minds filled with questions and wonder. The simple act of observing a tomato had opened up a world of scientific discovery, igniting their curiosity and inspiring a lifelong love of learning.

■■■

CHAPTER 52

WHY DO PEOPLE HAVE DIFFERENT SKIN COLOURS?

Aarika tilted her head, her small finger tracing the outline of her arm. "Papa, why do people have different skin colours?" she asked, her voice filled with curiosity.

Paarth, ever the inquisitive companion, joined the conversation, his eyes wide with wonder. "Yeah, some people are really, really brown, and some are really, really white!" he exclaimed.

Their father chuckled, a warm sound that filled the room. He knelt beside them, his gaze filled with gentle understanding. "That's a great question, my little explorers," he began, his voice laced with a hint of excitement. "Skin colour is like a beautiful rainbow, with many different shades."

Aarika's eyes sparkled with curiosity. "Like a rainbow after the rain?" she asked, her imagination taking flight.

Their father smiled. "Exactly like that, Aarika. Our skin colour is determined by a special pigment called melanin."

Paarth's brow furrowed in concentration. "Is it like paint?" he asked, his voice filled with wonder.

"In a way, yes," their father replied. "Melanin helps protect our skin from the sun's harmful rays. People who live in places with lots of sunlight tend to have more melanin, giving their skin a darker colour."

Aarika's eyes widened in understanding. "So, people who live in sunny places are like superheroes with built-in sunscreen?" she asked, her voice filled with admiration.

Their father laughed. "You could say that! But remember, all skin colours are beautiful and special. Diversity is what makes our world so interesting."

As they continued to explore the topic, a sense of wonder and respect for human diversity filled the room. The once simple question had opened up a world of fascinating discoveries, reminding them that differences are what make us unique and beautiful.

■■■

CHAPTER 53

WHY ARE CHILIES SO SPICY?

Aarika's eyes watered as she dabbed at her mouth with a napkin. “Papa, why are chilies so spicy?” she wailed, her voice filled with a mix of pain and confusion.

Paarth, the brave explorer, took a small bite of the chili, his face contorted in a mixture of curiosity and discomfort. “Yeah, it's like fire in your mouth!” he exclaimed, fanning his face with his hands.

Their father chuckled, a warm sound that offered little comfort to their burning mouths. “Ah, the fiery mystery of chili peppers,” he began, his voice laced with a hint of amusement. “It's all thanks to a special compound called capsaicin.”

Aarika's eyes widened in disbelief. “Capsaicin? That's a weird name,” she muttered, her mouth still tingling.

“It is,” their father agreed. “Capsaicin is what gives chili peppers their heat. It's a defense mechanism the plant uses to protect itself from being eaten by animals.”

Paarth's eyebrows furrowed in concentration. “So, chilies are trying to fight back?” he asked, his voice filled with a mix of awe and respect.

“Exactly,” their father replied. “It's nature's way of saying, 'Back off!'“

Aarika's eyes sparkled with newfound respect for the tiny chili. “They're like little spicy superheroes,” she declared, her voice filled with admiration.

Their father smiled. “Indeed, they are. But remember, even superheroes can be enjoyed in moderation. A little spice can add excitement to a meal, but too much can be overwhelming.”

As they sipped on glasses of cold water to soothe their burning mouths, Aarika and Paarth realized that even the smallest things in nature could pack a powerful punch. The fiery mystery of the chili pepper had ignited their curiosity and taught them a valuable lesson about balance and moderation.

■■■

CHAPTER 54

HOW ELECTRICITY IS PRODUCED?

Aarika's eyes widened in wonder as she watched the flickering television screen. "Papa, how does this box make pictures talk?" she asked, her voice filled with childlike curiosity.

Paarth, the curious companion, joined in, his eyes scanning the tangle of wires behind the television. "Yeah, and how does it light up?" he added, his voice filled with a sense of adventure.

Their father smiled and knelt beside them, his gaze filled with gentle understanding. "That's a fantastic question, my little scientists," he began, his voice laced with a hint of excitement. "This magical box, as you call it, works because of something called electricity."

Aarika's eyes sparkled with anticipation. "Is it like magic?" she asked, her imagination taking flight.

Their father smiled. "In a way, yes. Electricity is a form of energy that we can harness to do many things, like lighting up our homes, running our appliances, and even powering this television."

Paarth's brow furrowed in concentration. "But where does it come from?" he asked, his voice filled with curiosity.

"That's a great question, Paarth," their father replied. "Electricity can be produced in many ways. Sometimes it comes from water, like when rushing water spins turbines to generate power. Other times, it comes from the sun, using special panels to capture its energy."

Aarika's eyes widened in amazement. "So, the sun can make electricity?" she asked, her voice filled with wonder.

Their father nodded. "Absolutely! The sun is a powerful source of energy. It's like a giant battery in the sky."

As they continued to explore the concept of electricity, a sense of awe filled the room. The once mysterious power that brought their world to life had become a fascinating subject, a testament to human ingenuity and the wonders of science.

■■■

CHAPTER 55

WHERE DO RAINBOWS COME FROM?

Aarika's eyes sparkled with wonder as she gazed up at the sky, a vibrant rainbow arching across the post-rain horizon. "Papa, where does the rainbow come from?" she asked, her voice filled with childlike awe.

Paarth, her curious companion, joined her, his eyes scanning the sky for clues. "Is it a magic portal?" he suggested, his imagination running wild.

Their father smiled, looked at them "That's a wonderful question, my little explorers," he began, his voice laced with a hint of magic. "Rainbows are nature's way of saying thank you for the rain."

Aarika's eyes widened in delight. "So, the rainbow is a gift?" she asked, her face beaming with joy.

Their father smiled. "You could say that. Rainbows are created when sunlight shines through raindrops. The raindrops act like tiny prisms, splitting the sunlight into all the beautiful colours we see."

Paarth's eyebrows furrowed in concentration. "But how do the colours stay together in a circle?" he asked, his voice filled with curiosity.

"That's the magic of it, Paarth," their father replied. "The sunlight enters the raindrop at one angle and exits at another, creating a rainbow-shaped arc in the sky."

Aarika clapped her hands in excitement. "Let's find a rainbow every day!" she exclaimed, her voice filled with determination.

Their father laughed. "That's a wonderful idea, Aarika. But remember, rainbows are a special treat, a gift from nature after a rain shower. So, let's enjoy them while they last."

As they stood together, watching the rainbow slowly fade, a sense of wonder and magic filled the air. It was a moment they would cherish forever, a reminder of the beauty and mystery of the natural world.

■■■

CHAPTER 56

WHY DO STARS TWINKLE?

Aarika's eyes sparkled with wonder as she gazed up at the night sky, her finger tracing an imaginary line between two twinkling stars. "Papa, why do stars twinkle?" she asked, her voice filled with a childlike curiosity.

Paarth, the curious one, joined her, his eyes scanning the celestial canvas. "Are they winking at us?" he suggested, his voice filled with a mix of amusement and wonder.

Their father chuckled, a warm sound that filled the quiet night. He knelt beside them, his gaze filled with gentle understanding. "That's a fantastic question, my little astronomers," he began, his voice laced with a hint of magic. "Stars don't actually twinkle, you know."

Aarika's eyes widened in disbelief. "But they look like they're dancing!" she exclaimed, her voice filled with disappointment.

Their father smiled. "They do look like they're dancing, don't they? But the twinkling effect is actually caused by Earth's atmosphere."

Paarth's brow furrowed in concentration. "What's an atmosphere?" he asked, his voice filled with curiosity.

"It's a layer of air that surrounds our planet," their father explained. "As starlight passes through it, it gets bent and distorted, making the stars appear to twinkle."

Aarika's eyes sparkled with renewed wonder. "So, it's like the stars are playing hide-and-seek with us?" she asked, her imagination taking flight.

Their father nodded, his heart filled with warmth. "In a way, yes. The twinkling stars are a reminder of the magic and mystery of the universe."

As they continued to gaze at the night sky, a sense of awe and wonder filled the room. The once familiar stars had transformed into distant, twinkling companions, inviting them to explore the vastness of space.

■■■

CHAPTER 57
WHY IS THE OCEAN SALTY?

Aarika's tiny toes dug into the warm sand, her eyes sparkling with delight as she watched the waves crash against the shore. "Papa, why is the ocean salty?" she asked, her voice filled with childlike curiosity.

Paarth, the explorer, waded into the water, his laughter echoing as the waves splashed over his feet. "Yeah, it tastes weird," he agreed, making a funny face.

Their father chuckled, a warm sound that mingled with the rhythmic lapping of the waves. He sat beside them, his gaze filled with gentle understanding. "That's a great question, my little oceanographers," he began, his voice laced with a hint of adventure. "The ocean is salty because of the rocks on land."

Aarika's eyes widened in disbelief. "Rocks make the ocean salty?" she asked, her voice filled with confusion.

Their father nodded. "Over millions of years, rain has washed over rocks, picking up tiny bits of salt. This salty water flows into rivers and eventually ends up in the ocean."

Paarth's brow furrowed in concentration. "So, the ocean is like a giant bathtub filled with salty water?" he asked, his voice filled with wonder.

Their father smiled. "You could say that. The ocean is a vast and salty body of water that covers most of our planet."

Aarika's eyes sparkled with excitement. "Can we taste all the salt in the ocean?" she asked, her imagination running wild.

Their father laughed. "While it might be tempting, it's not a good idea to drink ocean water. It's too salty for us."

As they continued to play in the waves, a sense of wonder filled the air. The once familiar ocean had transformed into a mysterious and complex body of water, filled with secrets waiting to be discovered.

■■■

CHAPTER 58

WHY DO SOME PEOPLE HAVE LESS THAN OTHERS?

Aarika's small hand paused as she reached for a cookie in the cookie jar. Her eyes, filled with a mixture of curiosity and concern, met her father's gaze. "Papa, why do some people have less than others?" Her voice was soft, filled with a childlike innocence that belied the depth of her question.

Paarth, her observant companion, looked up from his toy car, his brow furrowed in thought. "Yeah, why don't they have toys like us?" he asked, his voice filled with a genuine sense of empathy.

Their father's heart ached as he witnessed their innocent concern. He knelt down, pulling them both into a warm embrace. "It's a big question, my little ones," he began, his voice gentle and reassuring. "The world isn't always fair, and sometimes people have less than others."

Aarika's lower lip quivered. "But that's not nice," she protested, her voice filled with indignation.

"No, it's not nice at all," their father agreed. "There are many reasons why this happens. Sometimes, it's because of where people live, or the opportunities they have. Sometimes, it's because of bad luck or unfairness."

Paarth's eyes filled with determination. "We can help them, right?" he asked, his voice filled with hope.

Their father smiled, his eyes filled with pride. "We can, Paarth. By being kind, sharing what we have, and helping others, we can make a difference."

Aarika nodded, her eyes shining with newfound understanding. "Let's share our toys with other kids," she suggested, her voice filled with generosity.

Their father's heart swelled with love as he watched his children, so young yet so compassionate. He knew that the seeds of empathy they were sowing today would blossom into beautiful acts of kindness in the future.

■■■

CHAPTER 59

WHAT IS A DREAM?

Aarika's eyes were wide with wonder as she stretched in her bed, the remnants of a vivid dream still dancing in her mind. "Papa, what is a dream?" she asked, her voice filled with a mix of curiosity and confusion.

Paarth, rubbing his eyes, sat up in bed, his mind still half-lost in a dream world of his own. "Yeah, I saw a giant dinosaur chasing me," he said, his voice filled with a mix of fear and excitement.

Their father chuckled, a warm sound that filled the quiet morning air. He sat up in bed, pulling them both into a comforting embrace. "Dreams are like magical movies that play in our minds while we sleep," he began, his voice gentle and reassuring.

Aarika's eyes sparkled with excitement. "Like a superhero movie?" she asked, her imagination taking flight.

Their father smiled. "Sometimes, yes. Dreams can be full of adventure, excitement, or even a little bit of scary stuff."

Paarth nodded, his face still bearing the marks of his dream. "But why do we have them?" he asked, his voice filled with curiosity.

"That's a great question, Paarth," their father replied. "Dreams are a way for our brains to process information and emotions. They can help us solve problems, or simply let our imaginations run wild."

Aarika's eyes filled with wonder. "So, dreams are like secret messages from our brains?" she asked, her voice filled with awe.

Their father smiled. "In a way, yes. They're a window into our thoughts and feelings."

As they lay back down, the children drifted off to sleep, their minds filled with images of their dreams. The boundary between reality and imagination blurred, and as they drifted into slumber, they carried with them the comforting knowledge that even in the world of dreams, they were loved and protected.

■■■

CHAPTER 60:
WHY DO PEOPLE GET MARRIED?

Aarika watched as her parents held hands, a soft smile playing on her lips. "Papa, why do people get married?" she asked, her voice filled with innocent curiosity.

Paarth, his eyes wide with wonder, joined the conversation. "Is it like a party?" he asked, his imagination running wild.

Their father chuckled, a warm sound that filled the room. He knelt beside them, his gaze filled with love. "Marriage is a special promise between two people who love each other very much," he began, his voice gentle and reassuring.

Aarika's eyes sparkled with excitement. "Like a superhero team?" she asked, her imagination taking flight.

Their father smiled. "You could say that, Aarika. Married people promise to support each other, to share their lives, and to build a family together."

Paarth's brow furrowed in concentration. "But why can't we just be friends?" he asked, his voice filled with confusion.

Their father took a deep breath. "Being married is like being best friends who promise to always be there for each other, no matter what. It's about love, trust, and commitment."

Aarika's face softened. "Like you and Mama?" she asked, her voice filled with warmth.

Their father nodded, his eyes filled with love. "Exactly like us, Aarika. Marriage is a beautiful thing, a symbol of love and commitment."

As they curled up together on the couch, the children listened to the soft murmur of their parents' voices, a symphony of love and companionship. The concept of marriage, once a distant and abstract idea, had begun to take shape in their young minds, filled with wonder and a growing understanding of the complexities of human relationships.

■■■

CHAPTER 61

HOW DO BABIES GROW IN THEIR MOMMY'S TUMMY?

Aarika's eyes were wide with wonder as she watched her baby cousin being cradled in her mother's arms. Her tiny finger traced the soft contours of the baby's face, her heart filled with a mix of curiosity and love. "Papa, how did the baby grow in mommy's tummy?" she asked, her voice filled with awe.

Paarth, ever the curious explorer, joined her, his eyes wide with amazement. "Did it come from a magic seed?" he asked, his imagination running wild.

Their father chuckled, a warm sound that filled the room. He knelt beside them, his gaze filled with a gentle understanding. "That's a wonderful question, my little explorers," he began, his voice soft and reassuring. "Babies grow in a very special place called the womb."

Aarika's eyes widened in disbelief. "A womb? What's that?" she asked, her voice filled with curiosity.

Their father explained, "It's a safe and warm place inside a mommy's body where a baby grows and develops."

Paarth's brow furrowed in concentration. "How does it get food?" he asked, his voice filled with concern.

"The baby gets food and oxygen through a special cord connected to the mommy," their father replied. "It's like a magical lifeline."

Aarika's eyes filled with wonder. "It's like a little underwater house!" she exclaimed, her imagination taking flight.

Their father smiled. "You could say that, Aarika. After about nine months, the baby is ready to meet the world."

Aarika's face softened. "I can't wait to have a baby," she said, her voice filled with a mix of excitement and anticipation.

Their father pulled them both into a warm embrace. “That’s a beautiful thought, Aarika,” he replied, his heart filled with love. “Growing a baby is a magical journey, filled with love and care.”

As they watched the baby sleep peacefully in its mother's arms, the children were filled with a sense of awe and wonder at the miracle of life.

■■■

CHAPTER 62
WHAT IS TIME?

Aarika stretched, yawning widely as she rubbed her eyes. “Papa, what is time?” she asked, her voice filled with a childlike wonder.

Paarth, still half asleep, sat up in bed, rubbing his eyes. “Is it when we eat breakfast?” he asked, his voice muffled and sleepy.

Their father chuckled, a warm sound that filled the quiet morning room. “That's a great question, my little philosophers,” he began, his voice gentle and reassuring. “Time is a funny thing. It's a way of measuring how things change.”

Aarika's eyes widened in confusion. “Like when I grow taller?” she asked, her voice filled with wonder.

Their father nodded. “Exactly. Time helps us understand when things happen and how long they take.”

Paarth's brow furrowed in concentration. “So, it's like a long, long line?” he asked, his voice filled with curiosity.

“You could say that,” their father replied. “We can measure time in seconds, minutes, hours, days, years, and even centuries.”

Aarika's eyes sparkled with excitement. “Can we travel through time?” she asked, her imagination taking flight.

Their father smiled. “While we can't physically travel through time, we can learn about the past and imagine the future. That's what makes time so special.”

As they sat together, sipping their morning milk, the concept of time began to unfold in their young minds. It was a mysterious and abstract idea, yet it was also a fundamental part of their lives. The ticking of the clock, the changing seasons, and the growth they experienced were all connected to this invisible force called time.

■■■

CHAPTER 63

CAN WE BUILD A TIME MACHINE?

Aarika's eyes sparkled with an otherworldly gleam as she gazed out the window at the passing cars. "Papa, can we build a time machine?" she asked, her voice filled with childlike wonder and a touch of impatience.

Paarth, the curious companion, sat bolt upright in his chair, his eyes wide with excitement. "Yeah, let's go to the dinosaur age!" he exclaimed, his voice filled with a sense of adventure.

Their father chuckled, a warm sound that filled the room. He knelt beside them, his gaze filled with gentle understanding. "That would be an amazing adventure, wouldn't it?" he began, his voice laced with a hint of magic. "Building a time machine is a dream many people have had."

Aarika's lower lip quivered with disappointment. "But can't we really do it?" she asked, her voice filled with a touch of sadness.

"Papa," Aarika unabated continued, her voice filled with a mix of excitement and doubt, "If we can't build a time machine, can we at least travel to the future?"

Their father chuckled warmly. "That's a great question, Aarika. In a way, we're already traveling to the future, one moment at a time."

Paarth, ever the inquisitive one, piped up, "But what if we want to skip ahead? Like, to the year 3000 or something?"

Their father smiled, his eyes twinkling with amusement. "Well, while we can't physically leap forward in time, we can learn about the future by studying history and science. Scientists predict that the future could hold amazing advancements, like flying cars and colonies on Mars."

Aarika's eyes widened in awe. "Flying cars? Wow!"

Paarth nodded vigorously. "And Mars! That's so cool!"

Their father continued, "Remember, the future is shaped by the choices we make today. Every decision, big or small, has the potential to influence the world around us."

Arika and Paarth exchanged excited glances. "So, we can help create the future?" Aarika asked, her voice filled with hope.

"Absolutely," their father replied. "By learning, growing, and working hard, you can contribute to the world in countless ways. Maybe one day, you'll even invent something that changes the future."

As the sun began to set, casting long shadows across the room, Aarika and Paarth were filled with a renewed sense of wonder and purpose. They realized that while they couldn't physically travel through time, they could embark on a journey of discovery and innovation, shaping their own destiny and the future of the world.

■■■

CHAPTER 64

WHAT WOULD IT BE LIKE TO LIVE ON THE MOON?

The night sky was a canvas, dotted with twinkling stars. Aarika's eyes, wide with wonder, were fixed on the moon, a silver disc hanging high above. "Papa, what would it be like to live on the moon?" she asked, her voice filled with a mix of curiosity and a touch of fear.

Paarth, her older brother, was already lost in his own cosmic daydream. "We could bounce like kangaroos!" he exclaimed, his eyes sparkling with excitement.

Their father chuckled, a warm sound that filled the quiet night. "That's a fantastic question, my little astronauts," he began, his voice laced with a hint of adventure. "Living on the moon would be very different from life here on Earth."

Aarika's eyes widened. "Would we float?" she asked, her voice a mix of anticipation and trepidation.

"Gravity on the moon is much weaker than on Earth, so you'd feel lighter, almost like floating," their father explained. "But don't worry, you wouldn't fly away!"

Paarth furrowed his brow in concentration. "But it's really cold there, right?" he asked, shivering dramatically.

"Very cold," their father confirmed. "We'd need special suits to protect us from the extreme temperatures and lack of air."

Aarika's face fell slightly. "No ice cream?" she asked, her voice filled with disappointment.

Their father laughed. "Well, we'd have to find a way to make ice cream in space, wouldn't we?" he replied, trying to cheer her up.

"Maybe we could use moon rocks to make special moon rock ice cream!" Paarth suggested, his eyes lighting up.

"Or maybe we could grow special space fruit that tastes like ice cream," Aarika added.

Their father smiled. "That's a great idea. And maybe we could have moon dogs, or moon cats, that can survive in space."

"And we could build a moon castle, with a slide that goes all the way down to the Earth!" Paarth exclaimed.

Aarika giggled. "And we could have a moon pool, filled with moon water!"

As they continued to gaze at the moon, their imaginations ran wild. They envisioned moon bases, spacesuits with built-in ice cream makers, and adventures among the craters. The moon, once a distant celestial body, had become a playground for their dreams, a place filled with endless possibilities.

■■■

CHAPTER 65

CAN WE TALK TO ANIMALS?

The warm afternoon sun streamed through the window, casting a golden glow on the room. Aarika's eyes sparkled with wonder as she watched the neighbor's pet dog, Buddy, wagging its tail. "Papa, can we talk to animals?" she asked, her voice filled with a childlike curiosity.

Paarth, ever the explorer, joined in, his eyes fixed on the cat usually curled up on the windowsill. "Can we ask them for treats?" he added, a mischievous glint in his eyes.

Their father chuckled, a warm sound that filled the room. He knelt beside them, his gaze filled with gentle understanding. "It would be amazing to talk to animals, wouldn't it?" he began, his voice laced with a hint of magic.

Aarika nodded enthusiastically. "We could ask the birds to sing us a special song!" she exclaimed, her imagination taking flight.

Paarth's eyes widened. "And we could ask the fish to tell us about the ocean!" he added, his voice filled with excitement.

Their father smiled. "While we can't talk to animals in the same way we talk to each other, we can learn to understand their body language and communicate with them in other ways."

Aarika's face fell slightly. "But that's not as fun," she pouted.

Their father squeezed her hand gently. "It might not be as magical as talking, but it's still amazing to learn about the animals around us and how they communicate. We can observe their behavior, understand their needs, and build a special bond with them."

"Like when Buddy wags his tail really fast, it means he's happy to see us," Paarth pointed out.

"And when the cat purrs, it means she's feeling content and safe," Aarika added.

Their father nodded. "Exactly. And when your friend Pritha's pet bird sings, it's like it's sharing a little piece of its world with us."

As they watched their own pets, a sense of connection grew between them. They realized that even though they couldn't speak the same language, they could still share moments of joy, companionship, and understanding with the animals in their lives.

■■■

CHAPTER 66

WHAT IF THERE WERE NO ADULTS?

The warm afternoon sun streamed through the window, casting a golden glow on the room. Aarika's eyes sparkled with a mix of excitement and fear as she looked around the living room, imagining a world without adults. “Papa, what if there were no grown-ups?” she asked, her voice filled with wonder and a touch of apprehension.

Paarth, his imagination already running wild, jumped up and down with glee. “We could do anything we want!” he exclaimed, his eyes wide with excitement.

Their father chuckled, a warm sound that filled the room. He knelt beside them, his gaze filled with a mixture of amusement and concern. “That sounds like a fun adventure, doesn't it?” he began, his voice laced with a hint of caution. “But there are many things adults do that we need.”

Aarika's enthusiasm waned slightly. “Like cooking food?” she asked, her stomach rumbling in agreement.

“Exactly,” their father replied. “And driving cars, building houses, and taking care of each other.”

Paarth's face fell. “We couldn't go to school or play at the park,” he said, his voice filled with sadness.

Their father pulled them both into a warm embrace. “It's important to have adults in our lives to help us learn and grow,” he explained, his voice gentle and reassuring. “They teach us important things and keep us safe.”

Aarika nodded, her eyes still filled with wonder. “But what if we could help them too?” she asked, her voice filled with determination.

Their father smiled. “That's a beautiful thought, Aarika. We can help by being kind, helpful, and responsible. Even small acts of kindness can make a big difference.”

Paarth chimed in, "We could help with chores, like setting the table or watering the plants."

"And we could help our friends and neighbors, like offering to share our toys or help them with their homework," Aarika added.

Their father nodded. "Those are great ideas. And remember, we can also learn from adults and show them our appreciation. A simple 'thank you' or a hug can go a long way."

As they curled up together on the couch, the children realized that while the idea of a world without adults was exciting, it was also filled with challenges. They understood the importance of the adults in their lives and the role they played in creating a safe and happy world for everyone.

■■■

CHAPTER 67

CAN I BE A SUPERHERO WHEN I GROW UP?

The sun dipped below the horizon, casting long shadows across the room. Aarika's eyes sparkled with another worldly gleam as she twirled around in her imaginary superhero cape. "Papa, can I be a superhero when I grow up?" she asked, her voice filled with a mixture of excitement and determination.

Paarth, the aspiring adventurer, joined in the fun, his tiny fists clenched in imaginary battle. "I'll be your sidekick!" he declared, his voice filled with enthusiasm.

Their father chuckled, a warm sound that filled the room. He knelt beside them, his gaze filled with gentle understanding and a touch of amusement. "That's a fantastic dream, my little superheroes," he began, his voice laced with encouragement.

Aarika's face lit up with a radiant smile. "I'll be Super Aarika!" she exclaimed, striking a heroic pose.

Paarth mirrored her stance, his voice echoing her enthusiasm. "And I'll be Super Paarth!"

Their father laughed. "You two would make a great superhero team. While you can't fly or shoot lasers, you can be heroes in your own way by being kind, helpful, and brave."

Aarika's eyes softened. "Like helping old people?" she asked, her voice filled with empathy.

Paarth nodded, his face serious. "And saving kittens from trees!" he added, his voice filled with determination.

Their father smiled, his heart swelling with pride. "Exactly. Being a hero isn't just about having superpowers; it's about making a difference in the world. And the best superheroes are the ones who use their powers to help others."

"We could help the environment by planting trees and cleaning up parks," Aarika suggested.

"And we could volunteer at the animal shelter and help take care of the animals," Paarth added.

Their father nodded. "Those are great ideas. And remember, being a hero also means being a good friend, a good sibling, and a good child. By being kind and respectful to others, you're already making a difference."

As they continued to play, their imaginations soared, fueled by the belief that they could be anything they wanted to be. The world, with all its challenges and possibilities, was their vast playground, and they were the heroes of their own stories.

■■■

CHAPTER 68

ARE THERE ALIENS EXISTING?

Aarika's eyes sparkled with a mix of excitement and fear as she gazed up at the night sky. "Papa, are there aliens?" she asked, her voice filled with wonder and a touch of apprehension.

Paarth, ever the explorer, joined her, his eyes scanning the vast expanse of stars. "Can we be friends with them?" he asked, his voice filled with childlike curiosity.

Their father chuckled, a warm sound that filled the quiet night. He knelt beside them, his gaze filled with gentle understanding. "That's a question that has puzzled people for centuries, my little astronauts," he began, his voice laced with a hint of mystery.

Aarika's eyes widened in anticipation. "Are they green and have big eyes?" she asked, her imagination running wild.

Their father smiled. "That's a popular image, but we don't really know what aliens might look like. We haven't found any evidence of alien life yet, but that doesn't mean they don't exist."

Paarth's brow furrowed in concentration. "Maybe they're hiding," he suggested, his voice filled with a sense of adventure.

Their father nodded. "It's possible. The universe is a vast and mysterious place, and there's a chance we're not alone. But for now, we can enjoy exploring our own planet and learning about the amazing life forms that live here."

Aarika pondered this. "Like those tiny creatures in the pond?" she asked, pointing towards the small pond in their backyard.

"Exactly," her father replied. "Even in a small pond, there's a whole world of life we can't see with our naked eyes. Imagine what might be out there, in the vastness of space."

Paarth piped up, "Maybe they're super intelligent and can travel faster than light!"

Their father chuckled. "That's a great idea, Paarth. Scientists are actually working on developing technology that could allow us to travel faster than light. But even if we could, the universe is so vast that it would still take a very long time to reach other star systems."

Aarika's eyes widened. "So, maybe aliens have already visited Earth, but we just didn't see them?"

"It's a possibility," their father admitted. "But we haven't found any concrete evidence of alien visit yet. It's a fascinating topic, and scientists are constantly exploring new ideas and conducting experiments to try to find answers."

As they continued to gaze at the night sky, a sense of wonder and possibility filled the room. The idea of alien life was both exciting and a little scary, but it also sparked their curiosity about the universe and our place in it.

"Can we build a spaceship one day?" Paarth asked, his eyes shining with excitement.

"Absolutely," their father replied. "We can start by learning about science, engineering, and math. Those are the building blocks of space exploration."

Aarika nodded, her mind racing with possibilities. "And maybe one day, we'll be the ones who discover alien life!"

■■■

CHAPTER 69

HOW DO ANIMALS KNOW WHERE TO GO?

The sun kissed the sky with hues of gold and orange as Paarth and Aarika, two curious nine-year-olds, sat swaying on their porch swing. The gentle breeze carried the sweet scent of freshly cut grass, and the distant chirping of birds filled the air with a serene melody.

“Papa,” Paarth asked, his voice filled with wonder, “how do animals know where to go?”

Aarika, her eyes sparkling with curiosity, nodded in agreement. “Like the birds that fly far away in winter.”

Their father smiled warmly. He loved sharing his knowledge with his children, especially about the natural world. “Well, you two,” he began, “animals have many ways of finding their path.”

Paarth's eyes widened. “Do they have maps?”

Their father chuckled. “Not quite, but they have incredible senses. Some can smell their way home from hundreds of miles away.”

Aarika's face lit up. “Like the dog that found its way back?”

He nodded. “Exactly. Others use the stars as their night-time guide.”

Paarth's imagination soared. “Can we see the stars from our backyard?”

“Absolutely,” his father replied. “Let's go out and look at them tonight.”

As darkness enveloped the sky, Paarth and Aarika lay on their backs, gazing at the celestial wonder above. They pointed out constellations and dreamed of distant galaxies.

“I wonder if animals can see the stars too,” Aarika whispered.

“I think they can,” their father replied, squeezing her hand. “Maybe that's how they find their way.”

As sleep claimed them, Paarth and Aarika felt a deep connection to the natural world. They knew that while they might never fully understand the mysteries of animal migration, they would always be filled with awe and respect for the creatures that shared their planet.

The next morning, armed with a magnifying glass and a notebook, they embarked on an adventure into the nearby woods. They discovered a hidden stream, a family of playful squirrels, and a vibrant butterfly fluttering among the trees.

"Look, Papa!" Paarth exclaimed, pointing to a bird's nest nestled high in the branches. "It's so high up!"

Their father explained, "Birds are excellent climbers. They have strong claws and powerful muscles that help them reach the highest peaks."

Aarika peered into the nest. "I wonder where the baby birds are."

Just then, a tiny bird fluttered out, taking its first flight. "It's learning to fly!" Aarika cried.

"It's a big step," their father said. "A rite of passage for a young bird."

As the day unfolded, Paarth and Aarika continued to explore, their curiosity growing with each discovery. They learned about the diverse types of trees, the intricate world of insects, and the creatures that called the woods their home.

When it was time to return home, Paarth and Aarika were tired but exhilarated. They couldn't wait to share their adventures with their mother and other family members.

That evening, around the dinner table, they recounted their experiences, their eyes sparkling with excitement. They spoke of the birds, the squirrels, and the butterfly, sharing their newfound knowledge of the natural world.

Their parents listened attentively, their hearts filled with pride. They knew that Paarth and Aarika had had a wonderful day, and they cherished their children's curiosity and love for nature.

As they drifted off to sleep, Paarth and Aarika dreamed of the woods, the stars, and the endless wonders of the natural world. They knew that their curiosity would forever fuel their exploration, and their awe would always be inspired by the beauty of the world around them.

■■■

CHAPTER 70

WHERE DOES THE WIND COME FROM?

The summer breeze rustled through the leaves of the old oak tree, carrying with it the sweet scent of wild flowers. Paarth and Aarika sat on the porch swing, their small feet dangling just above the ground. The sun danced on the ripples of the nearby pond, casting playful shadows on the grass.

"Papa," Paarth began, his voice filled with childlike wonder, "Where does the wind come from?"

Aarika nodded, her eyes sparkling with curiosity. "It feels like it's playing with us."

Their father smiled. He had always loved sharing his knowledge with his children, especially when it came to the mysteries of the natural world. "Well, Paarth and Aarika," he began, "The wind is like a big, invisible breath."

Paarth's eyes widened. "A breath?"

Their father nodded. "The Earth is like a big ball, and the sun heats it up. When the air near the equator gets hot, it rises up. Then, colder air from the north or south comes in to take its place. This movement of air is what we call wind."

Aarika looked up at the sky. "So, the wind is like a big hug for the Earth?"

Their father chuckled. "You could say that. The wind helps to keep our planet cool and healthy."

Paarth thought for a moment. "Can we catch the wind?"

Their father smiled. "That's a great question. We can't catch the wind itself, but we can feel its power."

As the wind picked up, Paarth and Aarika laughed as it ruffled their hair and sent leaves swirling around them. They felt a sense of freedom and joy as they danced in the breeze.

“I love the wind,” Aarika said, her eyes closed.

The man squeezed her hand. “I do too, Aarika. It's a reminder that even the smallest things can have a big impact.”

As the sun began to set, casting long shadows across the yard, Paarth and Aarika felt a deep connection to the natural world. They knew that even though they might never fully understand the mysteries of the wind, they would always be filled with wonder and gratitude for the beauty it brought to their lives.

The next day, Paarth and Aarika decided to make a wind chime. They gathered colorful bottles, string, and beads from around the house. With their father's guidance, they carefully tied the bottles to the string and hung the wind chime from a tree branch.

As the wind blew, the bottles clinked and chimed, creating a beautiful melody. Paarth and Aarika listened to the music, feeling a sense of accomplishment. They had created something beautiful from the power of the wind.

That evening, as they sat on the porch, they watched the sunset, the wind chime tinkling softly in the background. They talked about the wind, the Earth, and the wonders of the natural world.

“I'm glad we made the wind chime,” Aarika said. “It's a reminder of the wind's power and beauty.”

Paarth nodded. “And it's a reminder of how much fun we had making it together.”

Their father smiled. “It's also a reminder that we can create something beautiful, just like the wind.”

As they drifted off to sleep that night, Paarth and Aarika dreamed of the wind, the wind chime, and the endless wonders of the natural world. They knew that they would always be curious, always be exploring, and always be grateful for the beauty that surrounded them.

■■■

CHAPTER 71

WHERE CAN WE TRAVEL FASTER THAN LIGHT?

The summer sun bathed the living room in a warm, golden glow as Paarth and Aarika sat on the floor, surrounded by a scattered array of books and toys. Their eyes sparkled with a mix of curiosity and wonder as they turned to their father.

"Papa," Paarth began, his voice barely a whisper, "Can we travel faster than light?"

Aarika nodded, her eyes wide with anticipation. "Like in the spaceship movie we watched?"

Their father smiled, his heart filled with warmth. He had always loved nurturing his children's imagination and answering their endless questions. "Well, Paarth and Aarika, traveling faster than light is a fascinating concept, but it's a bit complicated."

Paarth's brow furrowed. "Complicated? Like the puzzle I couldn't finish?"

Their father chuckled. "Exactly. You see, according to our current understanding of physics, nothing can travel faster than light."

Aarika's face fell. "But what if we built a really fast spaceship?"

Their father shook his head gently. "Even if we could build the fastest spaceship imaginable, it would still be impossible to go faster than light. It's like trying to run faster than your own shadow."

Paarth's eyes filled with disappointment. "So, we'll never be able to explore other planets?"

Their father paused, his expression softening. "Not with the technology we have now. But who knows what the future holds? Perhaps one day, we'll discover new ways to travel through space."

Aarika's eyes brightened. "Like in a magic carpet?"

Their father laughed. "Maybe something like that. But for now, we can explore our own planet and learn all we can about the universe around us."

Paarth and Aarika nodded, their spirits lifted. They knew that even if they couldn't travel faster than light, there were still countless adventures waiting for them right here on Earth. As they continued to explore the world around them, they were filled with a sense of wonder and excitement about the possibilities that lay ahead.

Later that day, they decided to embark on a backyard adventure. Armed with magnifying glasses and notebooks, they set off to explore the wonders of their own little world. They examined the intricate patterns of the leaves, observed the busy ants scurrying along the ground, and marveled at the vibrant colors of the flowers.

"Look, Papa!" Aarika exclaimed, pointing to a caterpillar munching on a leaf. "It's so tiny!"

Their father smiled. "It may be small, but it's part of a big cycle of life. That caterpillar will eventually turn into a beautiful butterfly."

Paarth's eyes widened. "Really? How does that happen?"

"It's a magical process," their father replied. "The caterpillar will spin a cocoon around itself and transform into a butterfly. It's one of nature's greatest wonders."

As the sun began to set, Paarth and Aarika returned inside, their minds buzzing with excitement. They had spent the day exploring their own backyard, discovering new things and learning about the wonders of the natural world.

That night, as they drifted off to sleep, they dreamed of far-off planets, magical carpets, and the endless possibilities of the universe. They knew that even though they couldn't travel faster than light, their imaginations could take them anywhere they wanted to go.

■■■

CHAPTER 72
WHAT IS MONEY FOR?

Paarth and Aarika sat on the floor of their living room, surrounded by a pile of colourful coins and bills. Their eyes sparkled with curiosity as they turned to their father.

"Papa," Paarth began, his voice filled with wonder, "What is money for?"

Aarika nodded, her eyes wide with anticipation. "Can we buy a puppy with it?"

Their father smiled, his heart filled with warmth. He had always loved nurturing his children's imagination and answering their endless questions. "Well, Paarth and Aarika, money is like a magic tool that helps us get things we need and want."

Paarth's eyes widened. "Like the toys at the store?"

The man nodded. "Exactly. But money can also be used for other important things, like food, clothes, and a place to live."

Aarika looked thoughtful. "So, money is like a friend that helps us?"

The man smiled. "You could say that. Money can be a very helpful friend, but it's important to use it wisely."

Paarth reached out and picked up a shiny coin. "Can we make our own money?"

The man chuckled. "That's a great question, Paarth. We can't make our own money, but we can earn it by doing things like helping others or working hard."

Aarika's eyes lit up. "Can we help you with the gardening?"

The man nodded. "That would be wonderful. If you help me, I'll give you some money as a reward."

As they worked together in the garden, Paarth and Aarika felt a sense of accomplishment and pride. They realized that money wasn't just about buying things; it was also about hard work, responsibility, and helping others.

"I like earning money," Paarth said, his voice filled with excitement.

Their father squeezed his hand. "Me too, Paarth. It's a great way to learn about the value of things and the importance of giving back."

Paarth and Aarika felt a deep connection to the world around them. They knew that even though money might not be the most important thing in life, it was a valuable tool that could be used for good.

■■■

CHAPTER 73

HOW DO BABIES LEARN TO TALK?

The sun cast long shadows across the living room as Paarth and Aarika sat on the floor, surrounded by a pile of colorful picture books. Their eyes sparkled with curiosity as they turned to their father.

"Papa," Paarth began, his voice filled with wonder, "How do babies learn to talk?"

Aarika nodded, her eyes wide with anticipation. "I want to teach my teddy bear to talk."

Their father smiled, his heart filled with warmth. He had always loved nurturing his children's imagination and answering their endless questions. "Well, Paarth and Aarika, learning to talk is a magical process."

Paarth's eyes widened. "Like magic?"

Their father nodded. "Exactly. Babies start by making sounds like babbling and cooing. Then, as they grow older, they begin to understand the meaning of words and try to imitate them."

Aarika looked thoughtful. "So, we learned to talk by listening to you?"

Their father smiled. "That's right, Aarika. Listening is very important. The more you listen to others speak, the easier it will be for you to learn new words."

Paarth reached out and touched his cheek. "Does that mean we can learn to talk to animals?"

Their father chuckled. "That's a great question, Paarth. While we can't talk to animals in the same way we talk to each other, we can certainly communicate with them in other ways."

Aarika's eyes brightened. "Like petting them and giving them treats?"

Their father nodded. “Exactly. Animals can understand our actions and emotions, even if they can't understand our words.”

As they continued to explore the world around them, Paarth and Aarika felt a deep connection to the people and animals they encountered. They realized that communication was a powerful tool that could bring people together and foster understanding.

■■■

CHAPTER 74

WHY DO WE CRY?

The rain lashed against the windowpane, mirroring the storm raging within young Aarika. Her small frame shook with sobs as she clung to her father's leg. She was feeling bad, for her friend Geeta who she saw crying in school.

"Papa,"Aarika began, her voice barely a whisper. "Why do we cry?"

Her father, knew why she was asking this question, Paarth had already told him. He knelt beside her, his heart heavy. He knew the pain of seeing someone crying, that ache. He reached out, gently stroking her damp hair.

"Well, Paarth and Aarika," he began, his voice gentle, "Crying is a natural way to express our emotions. It's like our bodies' way of saying we're feeling sad, hurt, or scared."

Paarth's eyes widened. "But why do we feel sad sometimes?"

Their father smiled sadly. "Sometimes, bad things happen that make us feel sad or upset. It's okay to cry when you're feeling this way."

Aarika looked up, her eyes filled with hope. "Can we make the sad feelings go away?"

Their father nodded. "We can try. Talking to someone we trust, doing something we enjoy, or simply taking some time to relax can help us feel better."

Paarth thought for a moment. "So, crying is like a way to let the bad feelings out?"

Their father squeezed his children's hands. "Exactly. But crying can also be a sign of joy or happiness. Sometimes, we cry when we're feeling really happy or excited."

Aarika smiled. "Like when we won the soccer game?"

Their father nodded. "Exactly. Crying is a natural part of being human. It's a way to express our emotions and connect with others."

Today, they'd learned a valuable lesson: crying is a normal human emotion. They resolved to stand up for anyone who might be teased for shedding tears. They vowed to help others understand the importance of expressing emotions, no matter how difficult it might seem.

■■■

CHAPTER 75

WHAT IS A JOB?

Paarth's curiosity was piqued as he stood at the school reception. He overheard someone use a word he didn't recognize: "job." Intrigued, he pondered its meaning, the word echoing in his mind.

Back home, he couldn't wait to unravel the mystery. Bursting into his father's study, he blurted out "Papa,What is a job?"

Aarika nodded, her eyes excited about it. "Yes, I remember, someone asked me as well, "What job does your father do?"in the park a few days back."

Their father, was smiling at this innocent yet important question.

"Well, Paarth and Aarika," he began, his voice gentle, "A job is something we do to earn money and help support ourselves and our families."

Paarth's eyes widened. "Like the man who sells ice cream?"

The man nodded. "Exactly. People have different jobs depending on their skills and interests. Some people work as doctors, teachers, or artists."

Aarika looked up, her eyes filled with hope. "Can we get jobs when we grow up?"

The man smiled. "Absolutely! You can choose any job you like, as long as you work hard and learn new things."

Paarth thought for a moment. "Can we help you with your job?"

The man squeezed his children's hands. "Of course you can. You can help me with the gardening, or you can help me clean the house."

As they worked together, Paarth and Aarika felt a sense of accomplishment and pride. They realized that a job wasn't just about earning money; it was also about contributing to the community and making a difference in the world.

"I want to be a firefighter when I grow up," Paarth said, his eyes sparkling with excitement.

Aarika nodded. "I want to be a doctor and help people."

The man smiled. "Those are wonderful goals. Remember, with hard work and dedication, you can achieve anything you set your mind to."

■■■

CHAPTER 76

WHY DO WE HAVE DIFFERENT COUNTRIES?

The summer sun streamed through the shattered glass, casting a kaleidoscope of light across the living room floor. A globe, once a symbol of the world's wonders, lay in pieces, its map of countries now a fragmented puzzle.

Paarth and Aarika, their faces etched with curiosity, knelt beside the wreckage. Aarika picked up a fragment, her finger tracing the outline of a continent. "Why do we have different countries Papa?" she asked, her voice small.

Paarth, his eyes wide with wonder, pointed to a particular piece. "This is India, right?" he asked. "And this... this is America."

"Yes," their father confirmed. "And there are many, many more countries, each with its own story, its own people."

Aarika frowned. "But why can't we all just be one big country?"

Their father paused, his mind racing. He could have given a simple, textbook answer. But he chose a different path. "Imagine, if you will, a garden," he began. "A garden with countless flowers, each unique, each beautiful in its own way."

Paarth and Aarika listened intently, their curiosity piqued.

"Some flowers bloom in the sunlight, others in the shade. Some prefer the rain, others the drought. Each flower has its own needs, its own way of life. And just like these flowers, the people of the world are diverse. We have different cultures, different beliefs, different ways of living. But beneath these differences, we share a common ground: our humanity."

Aarika's eyes lit up. "So, even though we're different, we're all connected?"

Their father smiled. "Exactly. We're all part of the same garden, the same world."

"Well, Paarth and Aarika," he began, his voice gentle, "people have lived in different places for thousands of years. Over time, they developed their own languages, cultures, and traditions."

Paarth's eyes widened. "Like speaking different languages?"

The man nodded. "Exactly. People in different countries often speak different languages and have different customs. This is why we have so many different countries."

Aarika looked up, her eyes filled with hope. "Can we visit other countries someday?"

The man smiled. "Of course we can. It's a wonderful way to learn about different cultures and make new friends."

Paarth thought for a moment. "But why do people sometimes fight with each other?"

The man's expression became somber. "Sometimes, people have disagreements or misunderstandings. It's important to remember that we are all human beings, and we should try to treat each other with respect and kindness."

As the sun began to set, casting long shadows over the broken globe, Paarth and Aarika stood, their hearts filled with a newfound understanding. The world, with all its complexities and contradictions, was a vast and intricate tapestry, woven from countless threads of human experience. And they, as young and curious as they were, were destined to play their part in this grand, global story.

■■■

CHAPTER 77

WHY ARE SOME PEOPLE RICH AND OTHERS POOR?

The train screeched to a halt, spewing a cloud of exhaust into the humid air. As the doors slid open, a surge of people poured out onto the platform. Paarth and Aarika, hand-in-hand, navigated their way through the crowd, their eyes wide with the thrill of a new adventure.

As they were about to step off the platform, a wave of humanity washed over them. A group of beggars, their faces etched with hardship, surrounded the young siblings, their outstretched hands a stark contrast to the carefree vacationers.

Paarth and Aarika exchanged a worried glance. Their father, usually so calm and collected, seemed momentarily stunned. The sharp contrast between their comfortable lives and the stark reality of poverty was a jolt to their sheltered world.

"Papa," Paarth whispered, his voice barely audible over the din of the station, "Why are some people so poor and others so rich?"

Aarika nodded, her eyes fixed on the floor. "Like the man who lives in the big house and the woman who sells flowers on the street."

Their father sighed, his heart aching. He had hoped to shield his children from the harsh realities of the world, but it seemed their innocence was slowly fading. He took a deep breath and tried to find the right words.

"Well, Paarth and Aarika," he began, his voice gentle, "People have different circumstances in life. Some people have more opportunities than others, and some people have to work harder to make ends meet."

Paarth's eyes widened. "So, it's not fair?"

The man shook his head. "It's not always fair, but it's important to remember that everyone deserves to be treated with respect and kindness, regardless of their financial situation."

Aarika looked up, her eyes filled with hope. "Can we help people who are poor?"

The man nodded. "We can. We can donate to charities, volunteer our time, or simply be kind to others."

Paarth thought for a moment. "So, even if we don't have a lot of money, we can still make a difference?"

The man squeezed his children's hands. "Absolutely. The most important things in life are not material possessions, but love, kindness, and compassion."

As they walked away from the station, the image of the beggars lingered in their minds. The carefree vacation they had anticipated now seemed tinged with a newfound awareness. The world, they realized, was not as simple as they had once thought.

■■■

CHAPTER 78
HOW DO COMPUTERS WORK?

The rhythmic clacking of keys echoed through the quiet room. Paarth, his small frame perched on the edge of the couch, watched his father intently. His eyes, wide with curiosity, followed the swift movement of his father's fingers across the keyboard.

"Papa," Paarth began, his voice barely a whisper. "How do computers work?"

Aarika nodded, her eyes fixed on the floor. "Like the one we have in our room."

"Well, Paarth and Aarika," he began, his voice gentle, "Computers are like really smart brains that can do lots of things."

Paarth's eyes widened. "Can they think like us?"

The man smiled sadly. "Not exactly, but they can follow instructions and solve problems. They use tiny electrical parts called circuits to do this."

Aarika looked up, her eyes filled with hope. "Can we build a computer?"

The man nodded. "Not a big one, but we can build a simple computer using some batteries, wires, and a light bulb."

Paarth thought for a moment. "Will it be fun?"

The man squeezed his children's hands. "Absolutely. It's a great way to learn about how things work."

As they worked together to build their simple computer, Paarth and Aarika felt a sense of accomplishment and pride. They realized that technology was not just a magical tool; it was a product of human ingenuity and creativity.

"I want to be a computer scientist when I grow up," Paarth said, his eyes sparkling with excitement.

Aarika nodded. "I want to build robots."

The man smiled. "Those are wonderful goals. Remember, with hard work and dedication, you can achieve anything you set your mind to."

■■■

CHAPTER 79

WHAT IS A DREAM MADE OF?

The sun dipped below the horizon, casting the room in a soft, golden glow. Paarth and Aarika, wide-eyed and restless, had just woken from their afternoon nap. They were buzzing with an energy that only a summer day could inspire.

"Papa," Aarika began, her voice filled with a mix of curiosity and a hint of fear, "What happens when we sleep?"

Paarth nodded, his eyes mirroring her concern. "Like, when we dream?" he added.

Their father, a man of science and wonder, paused, his gaze softening. He knew the innocence of childhood was fleeting, and this was a question that could lead to a profound conversation or a simple, comforting lie. He chose the former.

"Well, my little dreamers," he began, his voice low and deliberate, "When we sleep, our bodies rest, but our minds... they journey."

Aarika's eyes widened. "Journey?" she echoed, her voice filled with wonder.

"Yes, journey," their father confirmed. "They travel to a place where time doesn't exist, where the impossible becomes possible. A place we call the dreamworld."

Paarth's brow furrowed. "But how do we get there?"

"It's a mystery, isn't it?" their father replied, a knowing smile playing on his lips. "A mystery that scientists and philosophers have pondered for centuries. But one thing we do know is that our dreams are shaped by our experiences, our hopes, and our fears."

Aarika's eyes sparkled. "So, our dreams are like little movies in our heads?"

Their father chuckled. "In a way, yes. But they're much more than that. They're a window into our subconscious, a place where we can explore the depths of our minds."

As the night deepened, Paarth and Aarika, filled with a sense of awe and anticipation, drifted off to sleep. They knew that tonight, their dreams would be more vivid, more extraordinary than ever before.

■■■

CHAPTER 80

WHY DO ANIMALS LIVE IN DIFFERENT PLACES?

The sun dipped below the horizon, casting the city in a warm, golden glow. Paarth and Aarika, their cheeks flushed with excitement, hopped out of the car, their tiny hands clutching their father's. The zoo, a world of wonder and mystery, had just closed its gates, leaving them with a lingering sense of awe.

As they walked towards their home, a quiet question hung in the air. "Papa," Paarth began, his voice barely a whisper, "Why do animals live in different places?"

Aarika, her eyes still sparkling with the magic of the zoo, nodded in agreement. "Like the polar bear and the monkey."

Their father, a man of science and wonder, paused, his gaze fixed on the darkening sky. He knew this was a moment to spark curiosity, not fear. "Well, you see," he began, his voice gentle, "it's a grand puzzle, a masterpiece painted by nature."

Paarth's eyes widened, his curiosity piqued. "A puzzle?"

"Exactly," their father replied, a playful glint in his eye. "Each animal is a unique piece, perfectly adapted to its own little corner of the world. The animals have different needs to survive. Some animals need cold weather to live, while others need warm weather. They also need different kinds of food and shelter. The polar bear, with its thick fur and blubber, is a master of the icy realm. The monkey, agile and intelligent, thrives in the lush, tropical forests."

Aarika's eyes lit up. "So, they choose where to live?"

Their father smiled. "Not quite. Their homes are shaped by millions of years of evolution. But they're also explorers, always seeking out new opportunities. Sometimes, they have to migrate, to travel long distances in search of food or better conditions."

Paarth pondered this. "Can we go on a safari someday?"

"Absolutely," their father replied. "We can journey to the heart of Africa, where lions roam the savanna and elephants roam the plains. It's a world of adventure and wonder, waiting to be discovered."

As they reached their home, the stars twinkled above them, a celestial map guiding the way. Paarth and Aarika, filled with a sense of wonder and purpose, knew that their journey of discovery had just begun. They would explore the world, one question at a time, unraveling the mysteries of nature and the universe.

■■■

CHAPTER 81

WHY DO PEOPLE GET ANGRY?

The wind whipped through the open car windows, carrying with it the scent of pine trees and distant rain. Paarth and Aarika, their faces flushed with excitement, were on a long-awaited road trip with their father. The sun beat down on the endless highway, casting long shadows that danced across the dashboard.

"Papa," Paarth asked, his voice barely audible over the roar of the engine, "Why do people get so angry?"

Aarika, her eyes fixed on the passing landscape, nodded in agreement. "Yeah, like when that guy yelled at the other driver at the gas station."

Their father, a thoughtful man with a gentle smile, paused before responding. "Well, you see, anger is a complex emotion, like a storm brewing inside a person. It could be because the person is feeling sad, frustrated, or hurt."

Paarth furrowed his brow. "A storm? But it's sunny outside."

"Yes, but sometimes, even on the sunniest of days, dark clouds can gather in our minds. When we feel hurt, frustrated, or afraid, these clouds can grow, and anger can be the storm that follows."

Paarth's eyes widened. "Like when I lose a game?"

The man nodded. "Exactly. Anger is a strong emotion that can sometimes be difficult to control."

Aarika's eyes widened. "Can't we control the storm, Papa?"

Their father smiled. "It's not always easy, but we can try.We can learn to weather the storm, my dear. We can take deep breaths, count to ten, find a quiet place to calm our mindsor talk to someone we trust. "

Paarth nodded, his eyes thoughtful. "So, like a captain steering a ship through a tempest?"

Their father chuckled. "Exactly, Paarth. We can be the captains of our own emotions, guiding ourselves through the stormy seas of anger."

The acrid smoke from the burning farm stubble hung heavy in the air, a stark contrast to the vibrant green fields they had passed earlier. Paarth and Aarika, their faces pressed against the car window, watched as the landscape transformed into a hazy, smoky expanse.

As they drove through this smoky veil, their minds drifted back to the day's earlier lessons. They remembered their father's words about the power of emotions, how anger, like a storm, could engulf us if left unchecked. They recalled the importance of understanding these emotions and learning to navigate them, much like a skilled sailor navigating a tempestuous sea.

With newfound wisdom, they looked forward to their journey, excited about the adventures that awaited them. They knew that, armed with the knowledge of emotional intelligence, they could face any challenge, weather any storm.

■■■

CHAPTER 82

WHY DO WE HAVE TO SHARE?

The neon lights of the movie theater flickered, casting an eerie glow on the faces of Paarth and Aarika as they emerged into the cool night air. The thrill of the blockbuster they'd just witnessed still coursed through their veins, but a new, unexpected tension hung between them.

"I want that chocolate bar!" Paarth declared, his eyes fixed on the vending machine.

Aarika, ever the peacekeeper, sighed. "But we agreed to share, remember?"

"Yeah, well, I'm hungry *now*," Paarth retorted, his voice rising.

Aarika in a motherly tone, "Sharing is a superpower, remember, Paarth?"

"But Papa," Paarth began, irritation in his voice. "Why do we have to share?"

Their father, who had been observing the exchange with a knowing smile, stepped in. "Well, my dear children," he began, his tone gentle yet firm. "Remember the hero in the movie? The one who sacrificed everything for the greater good?"

Paarth and Aarika exchanged a glance, their earlier excitement fading.

"He shared, didn't he?" their father continued. "He gave up his own desires for the benefit of others. That's true heroism, isn't it? Sharing is a way to show kindness and generosity.""

Paarth's eyes widened. "But what if I don't want to share?"

The man smiled sadly. "It's natural to want to keep things for yourself, but sharing can bring us closer to others."

Aarika looked up, her eyes filled with hope. "Can we share our love with everyone?"

The man nodded. "Absolutely. Love is a gift that we can share with everyone, no matter who they are or where they come from."

Paarth thought for a moment. "So, sharing is like spreading happiness?"

The man squeezed his children's hands. "Exactly. Sharing makes the world a better place."

"Sharing isn't just about material things," their father explained. "It's about giving of yourself, your time, your love. It's about making the world a better place, one act of kindness at a time."

A newfound understanding dawned on the siblings' faces. They realized that sharing wasn't just a chore; it was a powerful tool to create positive change. As they walked home, hand in hand, they vowed to embrace the spirit of sharing, not just for the sake of peace, but for the greater good.

■■■

CHAPTER 83:
WHY DO FRIENDS ARGUE?

The fading light of dusk cast long shadows across the playground, mirroring the somber mood of the two children. Paarth and Aarika, their faces streaked with dirt and sweat, sat side by side on a rusty swing set. Their father was walking and talking over the phone, with some of his business contacts. He had just hung up when Paarth asked.

He had just hung up when Paarth said "Papa", his voice barely a whisper, "Why do friends fight?"

Aarika nodded, her eyes fixed on the floor. "Like when we fight over toys."

This was something, their father had been observing from quite sometime. Their fights with their friends.

"Well, Paarth and Aarika," he began, his voice gentle, "Sometimes, friends argue because they have different feelings or opinions."

Paarth's eyes widened. "Like when we want to play different games?"

The man nodded. "Exactly. It's normal to have disagreements, but it's important to learn how to resolve them peacefully."

Aarika looked up, her eyes filled with hope. "Can we be better friends?"

The man smiled sadly. "We can try. We can listen to each other, apologize when we're wrong, and try to find a solution that makes everyone happy."

Paarth thought for a moment. "So, arguing is like a storm?"

The man squeezed his children's hands. “You could say that. Just like a storm, arguments can be powerful and scary. But it’s important to remember that storms pass, and so does anger.”

As they walked home, the setting sun cast long shadows across the path. Paarth and Aarika, their faces still flushed from the earlier disagreement, began to contemplate the nature of friendship. They realized that arguments were inevitable, but it was up to them to choose how to respond. By staying calm and composed, they could turn a potential conflict into an opportunity for growth and understanding. Slowly but surely, the twins were beginning to grasp the complexities of the adult world, one lesson at a time.

■■■

CHAPTER 84

WHAT IS A SECRET?

The wind whistled through the ancient neem tree, its gnarled branches casting eerie shadows across the moonlit garden. Aarika and Paarth, sitting in their garden, huddled closer to their father, their eyes wide with a mix of curiosity and fear.

"Papa," Paarth whispered, his voice barely audible over the rustling leaves, "What's a secret?"

Aarika nodded, her small hand clutching her brother's. "Like when you hide a surprise for us?"

Their father, a man of logic and reason, was momentarily stumped. This question, as old as time itself, seemed to defy a simple answer. He cleared his throat, "Well, my little ones, a secret is a special kind of knowledge, a piece of information that only a few people know. It's like a hidden treasure, waiting to be discovered."

Paarth's eyes lit up. "Like a pirate's treasure map?"

"Exactly," their father replied, a playful glint in his eye. "But instead of gold and jewels, secrets are made of thoughts, feelings, and dreams. They can be exciting, scary, or even a little bit magical."

Aarika's eyes, previously filled with curiosity, now held a touch of mischief. "Can we have a secret, just us?"

Their father smiled. "Of course, my little spies. A secret between you two can be a powerful bond, a secret handshake, a special code, or a shared dream."

Paarth thought for a moment. "Can we tell our secret to Mommy?"

The man squeezed his children's hands. "That's a good question. Sometimes, it's best to keep secrets between just the two of you. But if you feel like you need to tell someone, it's important to choose someone you trust."

As the wind howled through the trees, the twins felt a sense of excitement and anticipation. They realized that secrets, like the shadows cast by the moonlight, could be both mysterious and comforting. And they were determined to create their own secret world, a place where imagination could run wild and dreams could take flight.

■■■

CHAPTER 85

WHY DO PEOPLE GET OLD?

The water tap's leak in the kitchen and the echo of dripping water was making the quiet living room scary. It was a winter evening. Aarika and Paarth, twins of curious minds, huddled closer to their father, their eyes wide with wonder and a touch of fear.

"Papa," Paarth began, his voice barely a whisper, "Why do people get old and... and disappear?"

Aarika nodded, her small hand clutching her brother's. "Like Grandma. She was here, and then she wasn't."

Their father, a man of science and reason, was momentarily stumped. He'd always prided himself on having answers, but this question, as old as time itself, seemed to defy explanation.

He cleared his throat, "Well, you see, children, it's a bit like a candle. It burns bright and beautiful, but eventually, the flame flickers and dies. Growing old is a natural part of life, just like a flower blooming and then wilting."

Paarth frowned, "But why do we have to die. Why can't we just keep the flame burning?"

"That's a question even the wisest minds haven't fully answered," their father admitted. "But what we can do is make our light shine as brightly as possible while it lasts. We can fill our lives with love, laughter, and learning. And when our time comes, we can rest knowing that our light has touched others, and their light will carry on."

Aarika's eyes, previously filled with sorrow, sparkled with newfound understanding. "So, we're like stars, Papa?"

Their father smiled, "In a way, yes. Stars shine for billions of years, illuminating the darkness. And even when they fade, their light continues to travel through the universe."

Aarika looked up, her eyes filled with tears. "So we all will die one day. I don't want you to die."

The man pulled his children close. "I know, Aarika. It's hard to say goodbye to someone we love. But remember, even though Grandma, Grandpa is no longer with us, they will always be in our hearts."

Paarth thought for a moment. "So, we're like seeds that grow and then die, but our stories continue?"

The man nodded. "Exactly. Our lives are like stories that are passed down from generation to generation. Even after we're gone, our stories will live on."

As the last rays of sunlight faded, casting long, dancing shadows across the room, the twins felt a sense of peace wash over them. They realized that while the end was inevitable, the journey was what truly mattered. And they were determined to make their journey as bright and beautiful as the stars.

■■■

CHAPTER 86

WHY DO WE HAVE TO SAY SORRY?

The air crackled with tension, the once-cheerful living room now a battlefield of unspoken words. Paarth and Aarika, usually inseparable, sat apart, their eyes fixed on the floor. Their father, a man of few words, paced the room, his face etched with disappointment.

A heavy silence hung in the air, broken only by the ticking of the grandfather clock. The children had returned from school that afternoon, their faces flushed with excitement, only to have their joy shattered by a harsh confrontation.

"I can't believe you two would do something like this," their father's voice boomed, echoing through the room. "You've embarrassed us all. You should go and say sorry to Mr. Sharma"

Paarth and Aarika shifted uncomfortably, their guilt palpable. They had broken their neighbor's prized vase during a game of cricket, and the consequences were looming large.

"Papa," Paarth began, his voice barely a whisper. "Why do we have to say sorry?"

Aarika nodded, her eyes fixed on the floor. "We didn't break the vase intentionally, it was just an accident that happened."

"Well, Paarth and Aarika," he began, his voice gentle, "Saying sorry is a way to show that we're sorry for something we've done wrong."

Paarth's eyes widened. "But why do we have to feel bad about it?"

The man smiled sadly. "Sometimes, our actions can hurt others, and it's important to take responsibility for our mistakes."

Aarika looked up, her eyes filled with hope. "Can we make things better?"

The man nodded. "We can. Saying sorry is a way to apologize for our actions and try to make things right."

Paarth thought for a moment. "So, saying sorry is like a magic word?"

The man squeezed his children's hands. "You could say that. Saying sorry can help to heal hurt feelings and repair relationships."

Paarth and Aarika realized their mistake. They signaled at each other and together said"We're sorry, Dad," their eyes downcast.

Their father, surprised by their initiative, softened his expression. "I appreciate your apology," he said, "but actions speak louder than words. We need to make things right with Mr. Sharma."

With a newfound sense of purpose, Paarth and Aarika, along with their father, visited Mr. Sharma's house. They apologized sincerely for their mistake and offered to replace the vase. Mr. Sharma, initially angry, was touched by their remorse and accepted their apology.

As they walked home, Paarth and Aarika felt a weight lifted from their shoulders. They had learned a valuable lesson about taking responsibility for their actions and the power of a sincere apology.

As the sun began to set, casting long shadows across the room, Paarth and Aarika felt a sense of peace wash over them. They knew they couldn't change the world overnight, but they were determined to live their lives with kindness and compassion.

■■■

CHAPTER 87

HOW CAN WE HELP PEOPLE WHO ARE SAD?

The salty ocean breeze carried the distant cries of seagulls, a stark contrast to the quietude of the secluded beach villa. All of them, were on a Sea beach vacation. Paarth and Aarika, usually inseparable companions, sat apart, their faces etched with a newfound melancholy.

Aarika, was the first to break the silence. "Papa," she began, her voice barely a whisper, "Why are some people so sad?"

Her question hung heavy in the air, a stark reminder of the world's complexities. Their father, a man of few words, paused, his gaze drifting towards the horizon. "Well, Aarika," he began, his voice gentle, "sometimes life can be tough. People face challenges, losses, and disappointments."

Paarth, ever the curious one, interjected, "Can we help them, Papa?"

Their father smiled, a bittersweet expression playing on his lips. "Of course, my little ones. There are many ways to help people who are sad."

Paarth's eyes widened. "Like giving them a hug?"

"Yes, Paarth, that's one of the ways. Kindness, empathy, and understanding are powerful tools. You can offer a listening ear, a comforting hug, or even a simple act of service."

Aarika's eyes lit up. "Can we help the old man who sits by the temple every day?" she asked, her voice filled with hope.

"We can," their father replied, "but remember, true kindness comes from the heart. It's not about grand gestures, but small acts of compassion."

Aarika looked up, her eyes filled with hope. "Can we bring him some food or water?"

The man smiled. “That’s a wonderful idea. You can.”

Paarth thought for a moment. “So, we can be like superheroes for people who are sad?”

The man squeezed his children's hands. “You could say that. Kindness is a powerful force that can brighten someone’s day.”

As the sun dipped below the horizon, casting the sky in hues of orange and purple, Paarth and Aarika felt a renewed sense of purpose. They realized that even in the face of life's challenges, they had the power to make a difference, one small act of kindness at a time.

The next morning, armed with a bag of freshly cooked parathas, the siblings made their way to the temple. The old man, as usual, sat in the corner, gazing out at the people climbing the temple stairs. As they approached, he looked up, his eyes crinkled with a warm smile.

“Good morning, young ones,” he greeted them, his voice raspy.

Paarth and Aarika shyly offered him the parathas. “We thought you might like these,” Aarika said.

The old man's eyes widened with surprise and gratitude. “Thank you, dear children,” he said, taking the bag. “This is very kind of you.”

As they chatted with the old man, Paarth and Aarika realized that a simple act of kindness could bring joy to someone's life. They left the place feeling lighter, their hearts filled with warmth.

■■■

CHAPTER 88

CAN WE TRAVEL TO MARS?

The rhythmic hum of the ancient grandfather clock filled the silent room. Paarth and Aarika, their eyes wide with curiosity, sat perched on the edge of their seats. They were completing their school work. Their father, a renowned author and coach, was engrossed in a project report.

"Papa," Paarth began, his voice barely a whisper. "Can we travel to Mars?"

Aarika, ever the dreamer, nodded eagerly. "Like the astronauts in the books?"

Their father paused, a thoughtful expression crossing his face. "Well, my little explorers," he began, his voice a gentle blend of fact and fantasy, "Mars is a distant red planet, a world of dust and ice. But it's also a world of endless possibilities."

Paarth's eyes lit up. "Can we build a spaceship and fly there?"

Their father smiled. "Building a rocket ship is no easy feat, Paarth. It requires years of hard work, brilliant minds, and a lot of science.Scientists are working on it. It's a big project, but it's possible."

"Does that mean we can't travel to Mars" asked Aarika, disappointment all over her face.

"Well, Paarth and Aarika," he began, his voice gentle, "Traveling to Mars is a very difficult task. It's a long way away, and there are many challenges to overcome."

Paarth's eyes widened. "Like the aliens?"

The man chuckled. "Not exactly. The biggest challenges are the distance, the cold, and the lack of oxygen."

Aarika's brow furrowed. "And what about the aliens?"

Their father chuckled. "Well, while we haven't found any little green men yet, Mars is a fascinating place. It has towering volcanoes, deep canyons, and even signs of water."

As the day drew to a close, the siblings were filled with a newfound sense of wonder. They realized that the future held not just challenges, but extraordinary adventures. And perhaps, one day, they too could reach for the stars.

■■■

CHAPTER 89

WHAT WILL THE WORLD BE LIKE IN 100 YEARS?

The rain lashed against the windowpane, mirroring the storm brewing within Paarth and Aarika. They sat huddled together on the couch, their small bodies dwarfed by the imposing figure of their father. The room was silent, the only sound the relentless drumming of the rain.

"Papa," Paarth began, his voice barely a whisper. "What will the world be like in 100 years?"

Aarika nodded, her eyes wide with fear. "Will we still be here?"

Their father sighed, his gaze fixed on the distant horizon. He knew the answer, but he dreaded the thought of planting the seed of doubt in their innocent minds.

Their father sighed, his heart aching. He had hoped to shield his children from the harsh realities of the world, but it seemed their innocence was slowly fading. He took a deep breath and tried to find the right words.

"The world, my children," he began, his voice heavy with unspoken sorrow, "is a fragile place. It's hard to say exactly what the world will be like in 100 years. It is a place where hope and despair dance in an eternal tango." He paused, his eyes searching theirs. "In a hundred years, the world might be unrecognizable. It could be a utopia, a paradise where technology has solved all our problems. Or it could be a dystopia, a bleak wasteland where humanity has succumbed to its own greed and ignorance."

Paarth's eyes widened. "But what can we do?" he asked, his voice trembling.

"We can dream," their father replied, a flicker of hope in his eyes. "We can dream of a world where everyone is equal, where there is no hunger or poverty. We can dream of a world where we live in harmony with nature, where we respect all living things."

Aarika's lips trembled. "But what if our dreams don't come true?"

Their father pulled them closer, his arms wrapping around them. "Even if our dreams don't come true, we must never stop dreaming. For in the darkest of times, it is hope that keeps us going."

"So can we imagine a world with flying cars, robots that do our chores, and maybe even cities under the sea," asked Paarth.

"Yes, we can. Rather we should. Who knows we could become the future creators and protectors" said their father.

Aarika looked up, her eyes filled with hope. "Will we still have trees and animals?"

The man nodded. "I hope so. It's important to protect our planet and the creatures that live on it."

Paarth thought for a moment. "Can we help make the world a better place?"

The man squeezed his children's hands. "Absolutely. We can recycle, conserve energy, and be kind to others. Together, we can create a brighter future for ourselves and for generations to come."

As the storm raged outside, Paarth and Aarika clung to their father's words, finding solace in the shared dream of a better future. They knew that the world was uncertain, but they also knew that they had the power to shape their own destiny, one small step at a time.

■■■

CHAPTER 90

WILL THERE BE ROBOTS THAT DO EVERYTHING FOR US?

The rhythmic hum of the ancient grandfather clock filled the silent room, its ticking a stark contrast to the still, expectant air. Paarth, a curious ten-year-old with eyes that held galaxies of wonder, sat perched on the edge of his bed, his gaze fixed on the flickering glow of the bedside lamp.

"Papa," he began, his voice barely a whisper, "Will there be robots that do everything for us?"

Aarika nodded, her eyes fixed on the floor. "Like in the movie we watched."

"Well, Paarth and Aarika," he began, his voice gentle, "Robots are becoming more and more advanced every day. They can already do many things that humans used to do."

Paarth's eyes widened. "Like cooking and cleaning?"

The man nodded. "Exactly. But it's important to remember that robots are tools. They can help us, but they can't replace us."

Aarika looked up, her eyes filled with hope. "Can we build a robot someday?"

The man smiled. "That's a great idea. It's a challenging project, but it's possible with the right knowledge and skills."

Paarth thought for a moment. "Will robots take our jobs?"

The man squeezed his children's hands. "It's possible that some jobs will change, but there will always be a need for human creativity, problem-solving, and compassion."

Paarth's brow furrowed in thought. "Would they take over? Rule the world?"

His father chuckled, a warm sound that filled the room. “Perhaps, but not in the way you imagine. Machines, like tools, are extensions of our own abilities. They can help us, but as I said they can't replace the unique spark of human ingenuity and compassion.”

Aarika's eyes widened. “So, they won't turn against us?”

“Not if we use them wisely,”their father assured him. “Remember, the future is ours to shape. It's up to us to ensure that technology serves humanity, not the other way around.”

A sense of responsibility, mixed with a tinge of fear, settled in Paarth's heart. He realized that the future, with all its promise and peril, was not a distant dream, but a reality shaping itself before his very eyes.

As the sun began to set, casting long shadows across the room, Paarth and Aarika felt a sense of excitement wash over them. They knew they couldn’t change the world overnight, but they were determined to embrace the future with curiosity and optimism.

■■■

CHAPTER 91

WHAT IF THERE WAS NO GRAVITY?

The old mango tree outside the window swayed gently, its leaves whispering secrets to the wind. Inside, a different kind of storm was brewing. It was a quiet storm, born of a child's curiosity, a question that hung heavy in the air.

Paarth, a boy with eyes as deep as the ocean, sat at the kitchen table, his small hand clutching a half-eaten apple. His father, a man weathered by years of toil, paused mid-bite, a thoughtful expression settling on his face.

"Papa," Paarth began, his voice barely audible, "What if there was no gravity?"

The question hung suspended, a tiny seed of doubt planted in the serene afternoon. Aarika, Paarth's twin sister, tilted her head, her eyes wide with wonder.

"Like in those astronaut movies, where they float around?" she asked, her voice filled with a mix of awe and fear.

Their father chuckled, a warm sound that filled the room. "Well, Aarika, you're not far off. Gravity is a force that pulls everything towards the Earth. It's like an invisible hand, keeping us grounded.. Without it, everything would float."

Paarth's eyes widened. "So, if there was no gravity, would we float away?Like balloons?"

Their father smiled, his eyes twinkling. "Yes, Paarth, we would. We'd float like feathers in the wind. Imagine, no more falling down, no more bumps and bruises."

Aarika's eyes lit up. "Could we fly, like birds?"

The man's smile faded, replaced by a thoughtful expression. "It wouldn't be quite like flying, Aarika. We'd still need to propel ourselves, but it would certainly be a different kind of experience.You would need to use special equipment to move around."

Paarth thought for a moment. "Would we get dizzy?"

The man squeezed his children's hands. "It's possible. Without gravity, our bodies would be used to a different way of moving."

As the sun began its descent, casting long, dancing shadows across the room, Paarth and Aarika were lost in a world of endless possibilities. A world where the laws of physics were suspended, and the ordinary became extraordinary.

■■■

CHAPTER 92

CAN WE INVENT A MACHINE TO MAKE ANYTHING?

The rhythmic hum of the ancient generator filled the dim room, casting eerie shadows across the dusty walls. Paarth, his eyes wide with a mix of curiosity and fear, turned to his father.

"Papa," Paarth began, his voice barely a whisper. "Can we invent a machine to make anything?"

His twin sister, Aarika, huddled closer, her small frame trembling. The world outside their home was no less than a big mess. A big crowd was surrounding the transformer stationed at the corner of the street. Today their neighbourhood was a terrifying place, ravaged by a mysterious energy crisis. For the last two weeks, they were forced to live in the shadows, their lives dictated by the whims of the dwindling power supply.

Aarika nodded, her eyes fixed on the floor. "Like a magic wand?"

Their father, a science graduate, paused, his gaze fixed on the flickering light of the generator. The boy's innocent question was a stark reminder of the world they once knew, a world of abundance and wonder.

"Well, Paarth and Aarika," he began, his voice heavy with unspoken worries, "Inventing is a powerful tool, but it requires more than just imagination." He paused, his eyes searching his son's. "It demands knowledge, resilience, and a deep understanding of the world around us."

Paarth's eyes widened. "Like the scientists who invented the computer?"

Their father nodded. "Exactly. The computers and laptops that you know today have evolved. From being the huge-sized rooms to the sleek laptops that you carry in your bag, they have evolved big time, all with the innovative minds of the scientists."

Aarika looked up, her eyes filled with hope. "Can we invent a machine to make toys?"

Their father smiled. "That's a great idea. You could start by thinking about what kind of toys you'd like to make and how they would work."

Paarth thought for a moment. "Would we need a lot of money?"

Their father squeezed his children's hands. "Not necessarily. Sometimes, the best inventions are made with simple materials."

As the generator's hum grew louder, a sense of determination settled over the children. They knew that their future, and the future of their world, depended on their ability to innovate and adapt.

Later that night, as Paarth lay awake, a new idea sparked in his mind. He imagined a small, glowing device, powered by the energy of the wind and sun. It could light their way, and perhaps, even power their home. He whispered his idea to Aarika, who listened with wide eyes.

"We could call it a 'Hopelight'," Aarika suggested, her voice filled with excitement.

Paarth smiled. "A Hopelight," he repeated, the word echoing in the darkness. "That's perfect."

■■■

CHAPTER 93

WILL THERE BE FLYING CARS?

The morning sun kissed Paarth's face as he sat at his desk, a world of possibilities unfolding before him. A single sheet of paper, pristine and blank, lay before him, waiting to be filled with the ink of his imagination. His small hand, clutching a pencil, hovered over the paper, hesitant yet hopeful.

A soft knock interrupted his reverie. His father, a man of science and wonder, stepped into the room, his face etched with the lines of wisdom and experience. Paarth's eyes lit up, a spark of curiosity igniting within him.

"Papa," he began, his voice barely a whisper, "Do you think we'll ever have flying cars?"

His father paused, a knowing smile playing on his lips. "A fascinating question, Paarth," he replied, his voice filled with a hint of mystery. "Scientists are working tirelessly to make that dream a reality. But remember, the future is not just about flying cars. It's about pushing the boundaries of human imagination, about exploring the unknown, and about creating a world that is both sustainable and extraordinary."

Paarth's eyes widened with excitement. "Can we go to the moon, Papa? Like the astronauts?"

His father chuckled, a gentle hand ruffling Paarth's hair. "Perhaps, my boy. Perhaps one day, you and Aarika will be the ones gazing down at Earth from the lunar surface."

Later that day, as Paarth and Aarika frolicked in the park, their laughter echoing through the trees, Paarth couldn't help but ponder the possibilities. He envisioned a future where the sky was no longer a limit, where the stars were within reach, and where humanity had harnessed the power of innovation to create a world beyond their wildest dreams.

As the sun began to set, casting long shadows across the park, Paarth and Aarika sat on a bench, their eyes fixed on the twilight sky. A shooting star streaked across the heavens, a fleeting glimpse of cosmic wonder. Paarth's heart pounded with excitement. "Did you see that, Aarika?" he whispered. "A shooting star!"

Aarika's eyes sparkled with awe. "I wish I could fly up there and touch the stars," she said dreamily.

Paarth nodded, his imagination soaring. "Maybe one day we will," he replied, his voice filled with hope. "Maybe we'll build spaceships that can take us to distant galaxies."

As they walked home, hand in hand, Paarth and Aarika continued to dream, their minds filled with visions of a future that was both extraordinary and limitless.

.

■■■

CHAPTER 94

WHAT IF WE COULD LIVE UNDERWATER?

The rain pattered against the window pane, a rhythmic melody that lulled Paarth into a dreamy state. He was curled up on the couch, a worn copy of "Twenty Thousand Leagues Under the Sea" clutched in his hands. The story of Captain Nemo and his submarine, the Nautilus, had captured his imagination, transporting him to a world beneath the waves.

"What if we could live underwater?" Paarth asked, his voice barely a whisper.

Aarika, his younger sister, looked up from her drawing. Her eyes sparkled with curiosity. "Like mermaids?" she asked, her voice filled with wonder.

Their father, smiled. "Not quite like mermaids, but we could certainly explore the ocean depths. Imagine the incredible creatures we could see, the mysterious shipwrecks we could discover."

Paarth's eyes widened. "Could we build a submarine like Captain Nemo?"

Their father chuckled. "Well, not quite a submarine, but we could design underwater habitats where people could live and work. It's a fascinating field of study, and scientists are working hard to make it a reality."

Aarika piped up, "Could we have a garden underwater?"

Their father laughed. "That's a great idea! We could grow special plants that can survive in the deep sea. It's a challenging task, but with enough creativity and technology, anything is possible."

As the days turned into weeks, Paarth and Aarika's fascination with the underwater world grew. They spent countless hours researching marine life, designing their own underwater habitats, and even attempting to build a miniature submarine out of recycled materials.

One day, their father took them on a scuba diving trip. As they descended into the crystal-clear waters, a whole new world opened up before their eyes. Schools of colorful fish darted through the coral reefs, sea turtles glided gracefully through the water, and a majestic manta ray soared overhead.

Paarth and Aarika were awestruck. They had never seen anything so beautiful. The silence of the underwater world was broken only by the gentle lapping of waves and the occasional chirping of a fish. It was a world of peace and tranquility, a stark contrast to the hustle and bustle of their everyday lives.

As they surfaced, Paarth turned to his father. "I want to be a marine biologist when I grow up," he declared.

Aarika nodded in agreement. "Me too!"

Their father smiled. He knew that the seeds of curiosity and wonder had been planted, and that the future held endless possibilities for his children.

■■■

CHAPTER 95

CAN WE BRING DINOSAURS BACK TO LIFE?

Saturday afternoons, a sacred time for Paarth and Aarika, were usually spent nose-deep in books. But this summer, the usual routine had been disrupted. The relentless heat had forced them indoors, their air conditioners wheezing in protest.

Now, they lay side by side on their bed, their favorite Wimpy Kid books offering a much-needed escape from the sweltering heat. With each passing year, the summers seemed to grow more intense, confining them to the cool confines of their air-conditioned homes. Their father, too, was holed up in the living room, working on his latest project.

Something cropped up, and Paarth, his eyes clouded with confusion and fear, went to his father.

"Papa," Paarth began, his voice barely a whisper. "Can we bring dinosaurs back to life?"

Aarika who had followed him, nodded, her eyes fixed on the floor. "Like in the movie we watched."

Their father got a little taken aback. He'd always cherished the innocence of his children, their unburdened minds soaring through the vast expanse of imagination. But this question, so simple yet so profound, marked a shift. It was a poignant reminder that his children were growing, their curiosity extending beyond the familiar to the extraordinary, the fantastical.

A bittersweet smile crept across his face. He knew he couldn't just make up stories forever. So, he took a deep breath and began to weave not a tale but the truth.

"Well, Paarth and Aarika," he began, his voice gentle, "bringing dinosaurs back to life is a very difficult task."

Paarth's eyes widened. "Why?"

Their fathers smiled sadly. “Dinosaurs died out millions of years ago. Their DNA is very old and broken. It would be very hard to repair it.”

Aarika looked up, her eyes filled with hope. “Can we try?”

Their father nodded. “Scientists are trying to do just that. They’re studying dinosaur DNA and trying to find ways to bring them back.”

Paarth thought for a moment. “Would it be scary?”

The man squeezed his children's hands. “It could be. Dinosaurs were very big and powerful animals.”

The doorbell chimed, interrupting their deep dive into the prehistoric world. Their father realized it was time for their skating class.

“Do you want to continue this discussion later, or should we head out for skating now?” He asked.

In unison, Paarth and Aarika shouted, “later!”

They dashed to their rooms, grabbing their skating bags, eager to glide across the ice and then return to their dinosaur debate. As they slipped on their skates, a sense of excitement filled the air. They couldn't wait to delve deeper into the world of dinosaurs, their imaginations ignited by the possibilities of prehistoric life.

■■■

CHAPTER 96

WHO MADE GOD?

Paarth and Aarika were on a trip to their maternal grandma's place. Like every usual trip Sundays were reserved for the trip to the sugarcane fields, with their grandpa. Their father also accompanied them, almost on every occasion. This time too. The wind whipped through the ancient banyan tree, its gnarled roots clutching the earth like gnarled fingers. Paarth and Aarika, their faces etched with a mix of curiosity and awe, sat beneath its sprawling canopy. The rustle of leaves and the distant chirping of birds filled the air, a serene symphony that contrasted sharply with the profound question that hung between them.

"Papa," Paarth began, his voice barely a whisper, "Who made God?"

Aarika nodded, her eyes fixed on the intricate patterns of sunlight filtering through the leaves. "Is God always there?"

Their father was not expecting this question from the middle of nowhere. It was indeed a complex question. But like always he appreciated them.

"Well, Paarth and Aarika," he began, his voice gentle, "It indeed is a complex one. A question that people have been asking for centuries. It's a question that science and religion have tried to answer in different ways."

Paarth's eyes widened. "So, we don't know the answer?"

Their father smiled sadly. "Not exactly. Some people believe that God has always existed, while others believe that a higher power created the universe. It's a matter of faith and personal belief."

Aarika looked up, her eyes filled with hope. "Can we ask God a question?"

Their father nodded. "You can. Many people talk to God through prayer. They share their thoughts, feelings, and hopes with God."

Paarth thought for a moment. "Can we be good friends with God?"

Their father squeezed his children's hands. "You can have a special relationship with God. You can feel His love and guidance in your life."

The sun beat down mercilessly, casting harsh shadows across the tree. Paarth and Aarika, their faces damp with sweat, sat beneath its sprawling canopy. The air was still and heavy, and the only sound was the distant hum of insects.

Later as the sun reached its zenith, casting a blinding light over the landscape, Paarth and Aarika felt a sense of peace wash over them. They knew they couldn't change the world overnight, but they were determined to seek answers to life's biggest questions with open hearts and minds.

■■■

www.ingramcontent.com/pod-product-compliance
Ingram Content Group UK Ltd.
Pitfield, Milton Keynes, MK11 3LW, UK
UKHW021402190726
13845UKWH00028B/828

9 789334 147506